Price and Financial Stability

Rethinking Financial Markets

David Harrison

LONDON AND NEW YORK

First published 2018
by Routledge
2 Park Square, Milton Park, Abingdon, Oxon OX14 4RN

and by Routledge
711 Third Avenue, New York, NY 10017

Routledge is an imprint of the Taylor & Francis Group, an informa business

© 2018 David Harrison

The right of David Harrison to be identified as author of this work has been asserted by him in accordance with sections 77 and 78 of the Copyright, Designs and Patents Act 1988.

All rights reserved. No part of this book may be reprinted or reproduced or utilised in any form or by any electronic, mechanical, or other means, now known or hereafter invented, including photocopying and recording, or in any information storage or retrieval system, without permission in writing from the publishers.

Trademark notice: Product or corporate names may be trademarks or registered trademarks, and are used only for identification and explanation without intent to infringe.

British Library Cataloguing-in-Publication Data
A catalogue record for this book is available from the British Library

Library of Congress Cataloging-in-Publication Data
Names: Harrison, D. M. (David M.), 1955- author.
Title: Price and financial stability : rethinking financial markets / David Harrison.
Description: Abingdon, Oxon ; New York, NY : Routledge, 2018. | Includes bibliographical references and index.
Identifiers: LCCN 2017060375 (print) | LCCN 2018001458 (ebook) | ISBN 9781315098142 (eBook) | ISBN 9781138299146 (hardback : alk. paper)
Subjects: LCSH: Financial crises. | Uncertainty.
Classification: LCC HB3722 (ebook) | LCC HB3722 .H374 2018 (print) | DDC 332/.0415—dc23
LC record available at https://lccn.loc.gov/2017060375

ISBN: 978-1-138-29914-6 (hbk)
ISBN: 978-1-315-09814-2 (ebk)

Typeset in Times New Roman
by Sunrise Setting Ltd, Brixham, UK

Contents

	Preface	vi
1	A brief history of our time	1
2	Expectations, knowledge and prices	11
3	Beyond price	19
4	Savings, investment and liquidity	31
5	Models, theories and apples	44
6	Policy implications – finance	55
7	Competition policy	73
8	A new European capital market	84
9	Geopolitics	100
	Technical annex: Do we really need a new Bretton Woods?	110
	Index	114

Preface

Why are financial prices so much more crisis-prone and unstable than real economy prices? This book develops certain themes from an earlier book, *Competition Law and Financial Services* (2014), written mainly for those with some knowledge of competition law, and so somewhat technical. In this work I go much further into the problem of radical uncertainty and its impact on economics, which so concerned John Maynard Keynes. It seemed to me that while Keynes was right, and the future is unknown and uncertain, there was more yet to say on the subject.

In other branches of human knowledge, including the social and natural sciences, we accept the future is unknown and uncertain, and yet we get by. We do so by building theories which allow us to see over the horizon, around corners and a little way into the future; knowing all the time these theories may be wrong, but giving them our provisional acceptance until something better comes along. This scientific method is explained, so far as I know, by no-one better than the philosopher Karl Popper; and so this book looks at the economic problem of radical uncertainty from the perspective of Popper's theory of knowledge.

The bridge between the two is Popper's idea of expectations. Man is a problem-solving animal (in fact, Popper would say all life is problem-solving) and we increase our knowledge by the trial and error process of testing our expectations against the world we find ourselves in. It was Keynes' genius to observe that in economics there are two types of expectation: the short-term expectations of the producer when he wants to sell something; and the long-term expectations of the same producer when he wants to add to his capital equipment, through investment. From this we can get to Minsky's two-price system in the market economy, and the difference between real economy markets and financial markets. We can also see why the former can be stable and the latter can be unstable. And from this we can see why financial crises arise.

The real world policy problem is then what to do about it. Keynes was a problem-solving animal too, and the post-war global arrangement he left behind (admittedly not in the pristine form he conceived it) was known as the Bretton Woods system. This perished in its original form in 1971 at the hands of Richard Nixon, and the global economy has been spinning off its axis ever since. However, the Bretton Woods treaty arrangements still exist, at least on paper, and there is something to be said for seeing what can be salvaged.

Hayek (who was close to Popper) made the profound comment that the price system diffuses useful knowledge around the economy. But this only applies in the first, real economy, price system. The second, unstable, financial price system diffuses expectations, rather than useful knowledge. Those expectations shift, moment by moment, day by day, year by year, in line with moods and sentiment in investment markets, but not reality.

There may be other ways of solving this problem, but the suggestion I put forward in the book is that expectations of this nature need a standard to guide them, and that standard should be the public good of relative financial and asset price stability. Since the present unstable system is global, a global response is required, and the easiest method would be to use the Bretton Woods framework – which still exists – as a means to promote greater stability.

I am greatly indebted, for comments, criticism and encouragement, on all or parts of the book, to Edward Hadas, Robert Pringle, Jacques de Larosière, Philip Ward, Markus Reule, Andy Haldane, Paul Woolley, Kristina Abbotts, Nick Scarles, Anthony Teasdale, Stan Maes, Jeffrey Franks, Beatrice Heuser, my son Thomas and above all my wife Valerie Caton. An article from 2014 in the *Law and Financial Markets Review*, on which the chapter on a new European capital market is based, was greatly improved by Phoebus Athanassiou. (Jacques de Larosière very kindly commended it in a speech before the European Parliament in 2016.) I have, finally, framed a wonderful letter from a certain Jack Bogle of Valley Forge, Pennsylvania, enthusing about an article from 2015, entitled "The Logic of Price Discovery", sketching out a possible application of Popper's method to the problems of finance. (The article is now available via the Karl Popper Foundation, Klagenfurt, Austria.)

I felt suitably encouraged by all comments received to pursue the writing of this book; but of course no-one mentioned above is expected to agree with the final result, or the suggestions made. (I also have an email from Bogle, commenting on ideas for global monetary reform, observing "ideas are a dime a dozen: implementation is everything." Popper could not have put it better.)

Like Gandalf in the Shire, who refused to utter the language of Mordor, I have omitted to refer to "Brexit" in this book. While I can understand the discontents which led to the UK vote in 2016 (many of which flow from the subject matter of the book), the decision of the UK government to leave the EU can best be described as a detour from reality, which will not solve the underlying problems. Ending the post-war Bretton Woods global order in 1971 was a step backwards; opting out of the post-war European order now will not improve matters. It follows from the argument of this book that a more productive strategy for the UK would be to work with the rest of Europe to create a more stable global system, so that the crisis of 2008 does not repeat itself, and sufficient productive investment comes on stream to ensure decent growth and jobs. The proposal in these pages for a long-term European capital market as a motor for growth would be a useful step in that direction.

1 A brief history of our time

The political economy of the global financial order has come under intense scrutiny since the 2008 financial crisis. Opinions are divided. On the one hand, since the collapse of communism few still seriously doubt that the market economy in some sense "works", and that Adam Smith's division of labour is a better route to prosperity than anything else available. On the other hand, few doubt that the financial system in some sense does not. And when it is explained that the last financial crisis was not unique, but merely the latest and the largest of a series of unfortunate events, anxieties understandably multiply.

This book will look into the disjunction more deeply. Why is it that the market economy can process countless transactions over many decades involving real, every-day goods and services without blowing up, and increase the wealth and wellbeing of the nations which participate; and yet the same or very similar processes, when applied in the realm of finance, end up not adding to but subtracting from this same wealth of nations, with periodic crises?

Common to both the market economy and the financial system is the price mechanism, whereby participants buy and sell both normal goods and services and also financial assets. It seems, at first sight, as if prices must mean the same thing in both cases. And yet, this may be something of an optical illusion. Prices in the real economy are rooted in the real goods and services exchanged, passing from producers and sellers to buyers and distributors on their way to final consumers. Prices usually have a close link to costs, and there is generally a mark-up, or margin, over cost as items pass from hand to hand. Similar goods or services can be compared for value for money.

But prices in finance are not performing exactly the same function. In finance, millions of titles, or claims in the form of securities, pass from hand to hand, very often in large organised international financial markets, but the price of a transaction of this kind reflects more of an anticipation or estimate of the value of something else represented, such as an underlying asset. There is no relationship to costs, and in fact nothing is produced which can be costed: securities are really claims on streams of income from existing real items (like factories, or companies, or the debt of countries); or else they are claims on such claims (like derivatives).

Real economy prices are relatively stable, and do not normally oscillate wildly around central values. In recent decades, inflation, measured in terms of real economy prices, has been subdued in most of the developed world, with near price stability becoming the norm. But in finance, prices are, as a matter of course, much more unstable, whether we are looking at stock prices, currency values or derivatives based on financial values. Stock markets boom and crash in ways totally unlike markets for cars, or furniture, or computers.

It was the American economist Hyman Minsky who explained there are actually two completely different price systems in the market economy: there is one price system for the current output of current goods and services and the need to recover costs; and then there is a second price system for the values placed upon future income flows from outstanding financial and capital assets.

It is the instability of this second price system, valuing income flows from financial and capital assets, which is the heart of the matter, and the subject of this book. And when we look into it, this question turns out to be of more than just narrow economic interest. It is a basic question of political economy, touching on the organisation of our society, the very nature of knowledge and how we should best deal with a future that is always uncertain.

The open political societies we value are clearly suited to much in the modern world, including the exchange economy where there is trade in goods and services, nationally and internationally. Yet these societies, no matter how open and advanced, have still been buffeted by financial crises as seemingly blind and inexplicable as the Furies of antiquity, leaving winners and losers in their wake. Is this something inevitable that can only be endured, like the weather, or can improvements be made? Can this modern world be made more stable?

To help answer these questions, and to see the scale of the issues at stake, we need to look at how finance came to diverge from the real economy, when a shift took place several decades ago in the developed world, with the ending in the early 1970s of the post-war Bretton Woods global monetary and financial system.

An entire book could be written on the full geopolitical and economic consequences. In many respects, the world we live in now was set by a seemingly technical decision to break the link between gold and the dollar, taken in 1971 by US President Nixon with the aim of winning a second term in office. Until that date, and since the end of the Second World War, the gold price had been fixed in dollars at US$35 per ounce, and under the rules of the Bretton Woods system other currencies' exchange rates had been fixed to the dollar. (The precise gold/dollar rate predated the war, having been set by Roosevelt as long ago as 1934.)

The untying in 1971 of the world's monetary and financial system from a secure anchor led waves of instability to wash progressively through the world's economy, over the decades leaving hardly any political or economic order unshaken. Price signals became erratic and unreliable. Currencies shifted against other currencies. Commodity values (including that of gold) went up and down like yo-yos. Oil prices quadrupled, causing the disease of inflation to grip normal goods and services, until cured by a bout of extraordinarily high interest rates. The prices of capital assets – and financial prices generally – became detached from underlying economic reality, and instead became almost magnetically attached to each other. And no fewer than four waves of large scale international crises ensued, each one preceded by a credit bubble involving serious mispricing of financial and capital assets.[1]

Before we go on to look at the underlying and deeper causes, a brief review of what has happened in the decades since 1971 will illustrate the scale of events, in political and economic terms.

From gold to lead, and crisis to crisis: the 1970s

When the link between gold and the dollar was broken in 1971, there was an immediate impact on the price of oil, an essential ingredient in the world economy. It resulted in a sharp 70% decrease over the next two years in the price, *when expressed in gold*, received by oil-producing member countries of OPEC. This reduction in the gold value of oil they offset by a threefold increase in the *dollar price* in 1973, through the Arab oil embargo. Oil, a commodity whose price had remained relatively stable in the entire post-war period, now became volatile. By the end of the 1970s, a barrel of oil, when expressed in gold, had returned to not far off its price at the beginning of the decade: but it had increased by more than 800% when expressed in dollars.[2] To this day, volatility in oil and other basic commodity prices is quite normal.

The massive oil price hike (in dollars) ushered in the leaden economic years of the 1970s, in the US and Europe. Inflation, high unemployment and low growth took hold. The long post-war period of high growth and low inflation was over. Political instability grew. In the US, the near bankruptcy of the city of New York symbolised the chaotic economic backdrop. In the UK, the government, faced with industrial turmoil, called a general election on the question of "*Who Rules Britain?*" – and lost. Across Europe, political institutions were shaken by extremism and terrorist violence.

The increase in the dollar price of oil had the side-effect of greatly increasing the volume of dollars held by oil-producing countries, including dollars held in the accounts of large (mostly US) international commercial banks, operating in the offshore euro-dollar market. These large international commercial banks then recycled their dollar inflows ("petro-dollars") into new forms of lending, in particular to less developed countries without oil reserves.

In the course of the 1970s, commercial bank loans to governments and government-owned firms in Mexico, Brazil, Argentina and other developing countries grew at a rate of about 30% a year, and their external indebtedness increased by about 20% a year. This became the first major international credit bubble of the post-Bretton Woods era.

The 1980s

The build-up in private credit came to a halt in 1982, after US interest rates had risen in 1981 to 20% to combat domestic inflation and Mexico declared it could no longer service its debts. The flow of inward commercial bank credit stopped, there was a reversal in flows, and a serious Latin American debt crisis ensued, lasting for about a decade into the 1980s (a "lost decade").

The 1981 US interest rate rise epitomised counter-inflationary measures adopted throughout the developed world after the inflationary 1970s. The UK experimented with three different types of controls: first a prices and incomes policy; then domestic monetary targets; and then an exchange rate anchor. In the European Community the European Monetary System, launched in 1979, largely succeeded in re-establishing an island of comparative internal exchange rate stability over the next decade. Exchange rate realignments became less frequent and inflationary pressures were cooled by the alignment of monetary policies in Europe on those of the German Bundesbank, committed by law to a policy of safeguarding the currency.

As capital controls were lifted on the ending of the Bretton Woods system, financial innovation took off. In the first decade estimated daily turnover on the foreign exchange markets grew to become 50 times that on the New York Stock Exchange, in dollar value. Notwithstanding this (or perhaps because of it) currency fluctuation persisted globally. The dollar fell by 56% against the German mark in the period 1968 to 1979; rose by 81% between 1979 and 1984; fell by 49% between 1984 and 1987; and rose by 12% between 1987 and 1988.[3]

The low growth and high debt of the 1970s affected not only the developed world, and market economies. At the beginning of the 1970s the Soviet Union was still seen by some as a candidate to overtake the United States economically,[4] but as the 1980s drew on it too came under severe strain, with economic stagnation and mounting hard currency commercial debts in several Soviet bloc countries (Poland, Hungary and East Germany), as well as the Soviet Union itself. When Gorbachev arrived in power in Moscow in 1985 it was with a policy of restructuring the failing Soviet economy (through "perestroika") not abolishing it. However, the attempts at reform, involving the introduction of market measures into the command economy, led to political liberalisation and the eventual secession from the communist system by Soviet bloc countries, and finally the dismantling of the Soviet Union itself.[5]

Nor was all well in the market economies, even as communism collapsed. In the UK, liberalisation of the financial markets in 1986 ("Big Bang") preceded a major global stock market crash in 1987, the worst such crash since 1929. More long-lasting in its impact was the build-up of the Japanese credit bubble through the 1980s, the second major credit bubble in the post-Bretton Woods era. Deregulation of the Japanese financial system led to an increase in bank loans based on property, and property prices increased five to six times in the space of a few years. 1989 saw the fall of the Berlin Wall, appearing to confirm the triumph of market economics. But the following year, 1990, saw the collapse of the Japanese stock market and property-based credit bubble. Until that point Japan had been widely admired as one of the most advanced and innovative economies in the world. A long recession ensued, the effects of which are felt in Japan to this day.

The 1990s

The 1990s saw the market system consolidate in Europe, with several countries of the former Soviet bloc merging into it. The building of the European single market led on to preparations for a single European currency, but absorbing East Germany had a high interest rate cost in Germany, which created strains in the European Monetary System, leading to the debacle of UK exit in 1992 from the exchange rate mechanism, only two years after joining. The UK withdrew back into a policy of domestic inflation targeting, while continental Europe proceeded to the launch of the euro in 1999.

The decade of the 1990s, like the 1970s and the 1980s before it, had its own large scale credit bubble, this time mostly affecting the countries of South East Asia. Flows of money into China, Malaysia, Thailand and Indonesia, largely from Japan after the implosion of the earlier Japanese bubble, pushed up asset prices and currencies across the region. Stock prices, manufacturing activity and real estate values surged.

This bubble persisted until 1996, when consumer finance companies in Thailand began to experience large losses on their loans, foreign lenders to Thailand grew concerned and the flow of international money into countries in the region declined. In 1997 the Thai baht depreciated sharply, triggering a contagion effect so that within six months the values of currencies across the region declined by 30% or more, stock prices declined by 30% to 60%, real estate prices fell sharply and banks across the region failed. Increasing interlinkages between financial markets, and a tendency for investors to view emerging markets as an "asset class", caused ripple effects to spread internationally. There was a Russian rouble crisis in 1998, and the Russian banking system collapsed the same year.

One result of the consequent panic in the bond market in 1998 was the near-collapse of US hedge fund Long-Term Capital Management. In a dress rehearsal of the global financial crisis ten years later, this thinly capitalised financial intermediary, which had taken the wrong (optimistic) view of developments in the US bond market, had to be bailed out by a consortium of banks and securities firms put together by the Federal Reserve Bank of New York, on the grounds that not to do so would cause even further financial panic.[6]

Meanwhile, in Moscow, following the rouble crisis and collapse of the banking system Russian President Yeltsin unexpectedly resigned in 1999. He was replaced by one Vladimir Putin, who in 2018 (in his third term of office, plus a spell as Prime Minister) remained Russian President.

In South East Asia, political upheavals after the crisis included complete changes of regime in Thailand and Indonesia.

The twenty-first century

The fourth, and largest, credit bubble of the post-Bretton Woods era developed in the period 2002 to 2007 (a period of otherwise low interest rates and low inflation) and involved sharp increases in the prices of residential and commercial real estate across the world: in the US, the UK, Spain, Ireland, Iceland, South Africa, New Zealand and elsewhere. The increase in prices in the US was smaller than elsewhere, but concentrated in one third of the states, in some of which prices more than doubled. Although the mechanics of the sub-prime mortgage finance business were peculiar to the US, the common denominator was a rapid increase in the supply of credit to real estate. More financial innovation, in the shape of complex securities based on mortgage lending sold around the world, aided and abetted the process.

The tale of what happened next is now familiar. This fourth credit bubble burst when US real estate prices began to decline in 2007, leading to a collapse in the market for mortgage-related securities, distress in the US financial sector, the bankruptcy of Lehman Brothers and the spectacular near breakdown of the global financial system. Withdrawal of credit led to bursting of real estate bubbles around the world, a serious global economic recession and severe strains on public finances, made worse by the need to rescue the banking system. Sums estimated in 2009 to be equivalent to almost a quarter of global GDP were spent on supporting banks in the US and Europe.[7]

Casualties of the global financial crisis included the US itself, which endured the worst economic downturn since the Depression. In the UK, the first coalition government since the Second World War was formed to deal with the aftermath of the crisis. In the rest of the European Union, the large capital flows which had pushed up property prices in the euro-zone periphery came to a sudden stop, reminiscent of Latin America after the 1970s, and a long euro-zone crisis ensued.

In the extreme case of Iceland, where between 2002 and 2007 prices of residential real estate had doubled, stock prices increased by a factor of nine and assets owned by the three main banks increased from 150% to 800% of GDP, a sizeable number of bankers were convicted of criminal offences after the crash, and serious consideration given to the 1936 Chicago Plan, a scheme by US economists (never implemented) for complete public control of the creation of private credit by banks.[8]

The open society and its economics

It is now quite commonplace to compare and contrast the world since 1971, when Nixon broke the dollar's link with gold, with what went before. (Nixon won a Pyrrhic victory: he obtained his second term, but was soon engulfed by Watergate, and did not complete it.) The unstable system we have inherited appears both economically unsatisfactory and politically corrosive. Since the global financial crisis the developed countries have seen a notable surge in anti-establishment, extremist and isolationist rhetoric.

This is not surprising. Apart from the debilitating effects of a series of financial crises, economic growth has been less, inflation and unemployment higher, exchange rates more volatile and inequality within developed countries greater than during the Bretton Woods period.[9] The geopolitical consequences of successive shocks to established structures have been immense.

It is hard not to sympathise with the words of former UK Chancellor of the Exchequer Geoffrey Howe, as long ago as 1994:

> The quarter of a century between 1945 and 1971 now looks like some sort of economic golden age. For it was the period in which the world economy – victor and vanquished, developed and developing – experienced the most sustained and widespread growth in living memory. And not just growth but stability as well. Price stability, or something like it, was the norm by which we then lived.[10]

The argument which will be developed in this book is that behind the economic failings there lies a deeper conceptual, and indeed philosophical, problem. This helps explain why the market system "works" and the financial system does not. The Soviet economic system which collapsed under Gorbachev was genuinely worse than the western market economy model (as the clear evidence of the post-war division of Germany into two parts until 1990 attests). The shift in China to a market system has lifted millions out of poverty. But what we have around the world now cannot be said to be the last word in economic progress. Indeed, in terms of "sustained and widespread" global growth, it has been a disappointment.

The deeper underlying conceptual problem appears, perhaps surprisingly, closely connected to the incapacity of anyone, whether in open societies and market economies or anywhere else, to see very far into the future. This might seem a statement of the blindingly obvious. Yet the full implications do not seem to have been properly appreciated. In the post-war period open societies and market economies have developed strongly around the world, in a process termed "globalisation". In many respects this is very welcome, but there are consequences that need careful consideration.

In political and social terms, to borrow the language of pre-eminent philosopher Karl Popper, the future can be described as always open, and not determined by the past. In the open societies of today's world there are no iron laws of history, or "historicist" inevitabilities. It is impossible to predict the future growth of knowledge, and it is impossible to predict the future course of history.[11]

Popper is famous for writing *The Open Society and Its Enemies*, the great Second World War work of philosophy in support of democratic open societies, and against dictatorship, whether of the right or the left.[12] But Popper was also (and primarily) a philosopher of science, and his argument that the future is open was not limited to the social sciences. Even the best and most sophisticated natural scientific knowledge is tentative. The future of the universe itself is open.

In the language of a pre-war generation of economists like Frank Knight and John Maynard Keynes, the future is described, not as open, but as "uncertain", incapable of being reduced to any probability analysis or to a calculation of risks. There comes a point where the near future stretches into the longer-term future and, as to what might happen, as Keynes put it, "We simply do not know."[13]

Knight built a micro-economic theory of how firms operate in the economy on the assumption they faced fundamental (or, as it is now known, "Knightian") uncertainty.[14] Keynes constructed a macroeconomic theory of how the entire economy works, resting upon a similar premise. (Hyman Minsky said that Keynes without uncertainty is something like Hamlet without the prince.)[15]

To discount the inability to see very far into the future can have profound implications in the economic sphere, in particular where activities have a long duration, such as with the accumulation of savings or the use of savings for investment, which leads to future growth. The same applies to major macroeconomic developments, which evolve over a long time-scale. Yet, rather than drawing practical consequences for public policy of the severe limits of human knowledge, modern economic and financial theory has side-stepped the problem entirely by adopting simplifying assumptions of rational expectations and efficient markets. These assumptions have dominated mainstream thinking since the 1970s – a period characterised by low growth, instability and recurrent bubbles and crashes.

The assumption of rational expectations is that operators in a market economy, such as individuals and firms, have expectations of the future which are "rational", in the sense that the predictions they make are the best that can be made. Large complex macroeconomic models have been based on this premise since the 1970s, a period of research sometimes called the "rational expectations revolution".[16]

The assumption of efficient markets is that securities prices at any time fully reflect all available information, and these prices are reliable for investment decisions taken both by investors and firms themselves.[17] Although originally conceived for stock prices, by extension the same mode of thinking applies across the board in other financial markets, including currencies: the more trading there is of any financial asset the more information is incorporated in the price, and the more efficient the market.

Both sets of assumptions simplify real world market structures and interactions between firms to the point of abstraction, and remove uncertainty from the entire picture.

The curiosity is that, although modern economic and financial theory would like to think of itself as scientific, the rest of science does not work like this. As Popper pointed out, science proceeds not by putting forward hypotheses which can never be tested by experiment, but rather by putting forward theories which are capable of being disproved, or falsified.[18] Scientific theories are always tentative, and can never be proved by observation and testing – but they can be disproved. For economic theories to be "scientific" they should therefore not be dogmatic. They should be tentative, and they should be capable of being falsified.

It will be the argument of this book that since a fixed global monetary standard was abandoned in 1971 the loss of relative certainty of the future does much to explain financial price instability in a two-price market economy, and the resulting economic and political instability. When uncertainty is heightened, the relative certainty of what others (frequently competitors) can be observed to be doing now becomes more important, and subjectivity seizes liquid financial markets, too often with disastrous consequences. Instead of buyers and sellers opposing one another in competition over a financial price, everyone buys assets at the same time, or sells at the same time – the opposite of what is supposed to happen in the market economy. There is no division of labour, as in the real economy, which would cause the economy to grow, but instead a duplication of effort, with nothing new produced. The wealth of nations is not increased.

Many market operators have come to expect this, and take positions accordingly, in "momentum" trading, where the essence of success is timing the short-term movements of asset prices. If enough operators do this, movements in prices become self-fulfilling prophecies. But these self-fulfilling prophecies do not relate to the real world. In the case of currencies, since a global standard has been abandoned, and since nearly all foreign currency supply and demand arises within the inter-bank market, it is expectations arising almost entirely within this inter-bank market which determine prices. At one time it was supposed that a better currency system would result, and even that an "information standard" might become the new global standard, after Bretton Woods. What happened instead is that shifts in expectations create shifting prices and a moving standard, which, in the end, represents no standard at all.

Stability of real economy prices is usually seen as a public good, and institutions and policies exist to promote it. But it is the instability of financial prices which has been the greater problem in recent decades. Just as periods of high inflation undermine confidence in political institutions, financial instability insidiously shifts the ground beneath our feet, distorting perspectives and fracturing certainties. Restoring stability here could be a public good too.

To say that the future is "open", or that it is "uncertain", is important, but only the beginning. Neither the philosopher Popper nor economists like Knight and Keynes left matters there. The future still has to be faced, and decisions taken today which will affect tomorrow. How, therefore, do we get around the fundamental problem that we never know today what tomorrow will bring?

The answer, as the next chapter will explain, is that in practice we do always have expectations of the future – but those expectations may sometimes be right and sometimes be wrong.

Notes

1 Kindleberger C and Aliber R, *Manias, Panics and Crashes*, 2011, New York, Palgrave MacMillan.
2 Hammes D and Wills D, "Black Gold: The End of Bretton Woods and the Oil Price Shocks of the 1970s", Spring 2005, *The Independent Review*, IX, 4: pages 501–511. See also Authers J, *The Fearful Rise of Markets*, 2010, London, Financial Times Prentice Hall, page 32.
3 Figures from Robert Triffin figures in Guyot J, *Avant Qu'il Ne Soit Trop Tard*, 1991, Paris, Fondation Hippocrène.
4 Samuelson P, *Economics*, 1970, New York, McGraw-Hill.
5 Attali J, *Europe(s)*, 1994, Paris, Fayard.
6 Jickling M, "Lessons of Long-Term Capital Management and Amaranth Advisors", Chapter 11, Athanassiou P (Ed.), *Research Handbook on Hedge Funds, Private Equity and Alternative Investments*, 2012, Cheltenham, Edward Elgar.
7 Haldane A, "Banking on the State", 2009, *Bank for International Settlements Review*, 139.
8 Sigurjonsson F, "Monetary Reform: A Better Monetary System for Iceland", 2015, Report commissioned by the Prime Minister of Iceland.

9 Skidelsky R, *Keynes, The Return of the Master*, 2010, London, Penguin; Piketty T, *Capital in the Twenty-First Century*, 2014, Cambridge, Massachusetts, Belknap; and Bush O, Farrant K and Wright M, "Reform of the International Monetary and Financial System", 2011, Bank of England Financial Stability Paper No. 13.
10 Howe G, *Conflict of Loyalty*, 1994, London, Macmillan, page 161.
11 Popper K, *The Poverty of Historicism*, 1957, 1991, London, Routledge.
12 Popper K, *The Open Society and Its Enemies*, 1971, Princeton, New Jersey, Princeton University Press.
13 Keynes, JM, "The General Theory of Employment", 1937, Skidelsky R (Ed.), *The Essential Keynes*, 2015, London, Penguin, page 265.
14 Knight F, *Risk, Uncertainty and Profit*, 1921, Boston, Houghton Mifflin.
15 Minsky H, *John Maynard Keynes*, 1975, 2008, New York, McGraw-Hill, page 55.
16 Blanchard O, Amighini A and Giavazzi F, *Macroeconomics: A European Perspective*, 2010, Harlow, Financial Times Prentice Hall, page 355.
17 Fama E, "Efficient Capital Markets: A Review of Theory and Empirical Work", 1970, *Journal of Finance*, 25:2: pages 383–417.
18 Popper K, *The Logic of Scientific Discovery*, 1959, 1992, London, Routledge.

2 Expectations, knowledge and prices

In his book *The End of Alchemy (2016)*, reflecting on the origins and nature of financial crises, former Governor of the Bank of England Mervyn King recommends a switch in economic thinking away from modern risk-based calculations of utility based on probabilities, towards a recognition that "radical uncertainty" has its place too, and that new events can and do take place to which no probabilities can be assigned beforehand.

By "radical uncertainty" King means therefore much the same as Knight and Keynes. Beyond a certain point the future is not calculable. There exists "uncertainty so profound that it is impossible to represent the future in terms of a knowable and exhaustive list of outcomes to which we can attach probability."[1] According to King, failure to incorporate radical uncertainty into economic theories was partly responsible for the misjudgements that led to the latest crisis. And faced with radical uncertainty, operators in market economies fall back on "coping strategies", which for investors include shared narratives. Under radical uncertainty, market prices are determined, not by objective fundamentals, but by "narratives about fundamentals".

In this chapter we will consider this kind of radical uncertainty in more detail, and put it into context. While it is true that the future is unknown, this is by no means limited to the world of economics. Uncertainty applies across the board in many other human endeavours, including other social and natural sciences. It is not so much by espousing uncertainty that market economics becomes unique, or uniquely difficult: it is more that by doing so it reverts to the same position as other forms of science and knowledge, which have to deal with an uncertain future all the time. The creation of knowledge itself is a battle against uncertainty. So how is this battle fought in other fields?

The writings of Karl Popper provide perhaps the fullest explanation.

Einstein and the amoeba

Popper, in the course of his long philosophical career, built up what he called an "evolutionary theory of knowledge". It provides a comprehensive account of the way in which human knowledge, including scientific knowledge, has developed.

In simple terms, according to Popper all organisms have expectations of the environment or world in which they live. Some expectations are based on previous experience, and some (in fact, Popper thought probably most) are inborn, and unconscious, and result from the adaptation of an organism to the regularities of its environment. He uses as an example the development of a light-sensitive organ in the earliest single cell micro-organisms to be able to detect sunlight as a source of food. This light-sensitive organ eventually evolved into the eye, and allowed successor organisms to move into sunlight and also to avoid too much dangerous exposure to it, by a process of trial and error.

Knowledge grows from such a testing of expectations against reality – in particular where expectations prove to be incorrect, because the world does not do what was expected of it. At its most developed and sophisticated, scientific knowledge involves the creation of theories which can explain in great detail why an expectation was incorrect, and how a new theory which better explains the facts might be tested by experiment. But animals have expectations and knowledge in the same way as humans, and can also learn from their mistakes. As the title of one of Popper's books has it: *All Life is Problem Solving*.[2] Popper was fond of saying that from the amoeba to Einstein is only one step. Both work with the method of trial and error, but, unlike the amoeba, Einstein can create theories that live and die instead of him.

So holding expectations about the future, whether correct or incorrect, conscious or unconscious, is the normal human condition. This extends from an expectation that the sun will rise tomorrow to an expectation that a train will arrive at a railway station at a particular time. Neither, strictly speaking, is a certainty (and human knowledge would certainly be increased if the sun did not rise tomorrow) but such expectations are routine and reasonable, and indeed essential for society to function.

Scientific theories distinguish themselves from expectations and other forms of knowledge by being testable (or, as Popper put it, "falsifiable"). A scientific theory must contain some proposition by which it can be judged, not only by whoever puts forward the theory but by other scientists, in replicable experiments. A scientific theory can never be proved to be correct for all time but it can be proved to be incorrect, by experiment and falsification. Once it is proved incorrect, a better theory will explain why it is incorrect, until it, too, meets a new unexplained phenomenon which calls again for a better theory. Each new theory must contain the previous theories it replaces (so it must explain the same phenomena) and also explain the new, unexplained, phenomenon. All scientific theories, even the best and most convincing, are tentative, remaining the best only provisionally.

It can be seen why Popper called this an evolutionary theory of knowledge. Although he was interested in the underlying principles of the theory of knowledge (a branch of philosophy known as "epistemology"), Popper applied those principles to many scientific disciplines, writing in detail on subjects as diverse as evolutionary theory, neuroscience, cosmology and quantum mechanics.[3]

The line of demarcation between science and non-science (or "pseudo-science", as Popper termed it) is whether a theory is capable of being tested, or falsified.

Some ideas, conjectures or hypotheses cannot be tested, or falsified, and so have a status akin to myths, metaphysics and pseudo-science. Some pseudo-scientific ideas (astrology) may graduate into science (astronomy), as theories become testable, or falsifiable, perhaps through better technology.

Putting the whole Popperian picture together, we can say that we always have expectations about an uncertain future, based partly on previous experience and partly on inborn biological characteristics (such as our bodies being adapted to the rising and setting of the sun); that these expectations may or may not be correct, and are checked by a process of trial and error, by which our knowledge grows; and that scientific knowledge is only a better form of such knowledge because it can be expressed in the form of theories which can objectively be tested by others, to see if they are false.

The world of economics

Although Popper did not himself do so in any detail, we can, as we shall see, apply a similar approach in the field of economics. The future here too is open and uncertain, and not determined by the past. Nonetheless, expectations do exist, based largely on previously observed regularities. These expectations are not necessarily correct: they need testing by a process of trial and error.

In much of the market economy, with a division of labour, as described by Adam Smith, the price mechanism is in practice the best way to test expectations. There may be an expectation that a particular item produced at a particular cost might achieve a particular sale price, but no certainty until a transaction takes place. This is the basis of exchange in a market system. Expectations are tempered by the trial and error process of the price mechanism.

In *Risk, Uncertainty and Profit*, published in 1921, the economist Frank Knight made this kind of uncertainty integral to the market economy. According to Knight, it is not calculable risk which creates economic profits which are exploited by entrepreneurs, but genuine uncertainty of an unknown future. Knight distinguished between risk, as a quantity susceptible of measurement, and uncertainty, which is not. It is uncertainty of this nature which forms the basis of Knight's theory of profit, and accounts for the divergence between competition in reality and theoretical (or perfect) competition. The existence of true uncertainty prevents the theoretically perfect working out of the tendency of competition; gives the characteristic form of "enterprise" to economic organisation as a whole; and also accounts for the income of the entrepreneur.

Entrepreneurs must deal with aspects of uncertainty all the time. As Knight pointed out:

> It will be observed that the main uncertainty which affects the entrepreneur is that connected with the sale price of his product. His position in the price system is typically that of a purchaser of productive services at present prices to convert into finished goods for sale at the prices prevailing when the operation is finished. There is no uncertainty as to the prices of the things he buys.

He bears the technological uncertainty as to the amount of physical product he will secure, but the probable error in calculations of this sort is generally not large; the gamble is in the price factor in relation to the product.[4]

Knight laid stress on the fact that the ordinary decisions of everyday economic life are not based on perfect knowledge, but rather on estimates of a crude and superficial character. The normal economic situation involves an entrepreneur having an opinion as to an outcome, within more or less narrow limits. If he is inclined to make a venture, this opinion is either an expectation of a certain definite gain, or a belief in the real probability of a larger one. As Knight put it, "At the bottom of the uncertainty problem in economics is the forward-looking character of the economic process itself."

Expectations in the face of an uncertain future also play a major role in *The General Theory of Employment, Interest and Money* (1936), by John Maynard Keynes. Two entire chapters are devoted to the subject: Chapter Five ("Expectation as Determining Output and Employment") and Chapter Twelve ("The State of Long-Term Expectation").

The key point is made by Keynes at the outset of Chapter Five, in terms similar to Knight. All production is for the purpose of ultimately satisfying a consumer, but time usually elapses between the incurring of costs by a producer and the purchase of output by the ultimate consumer. The entrepreneur has to form the best expectations he can as to what consumers will be prepared to pay when he is ready to supply them after the elapse of what may be a lengthy period. An entrepreneur has no choice but to be guided by these expectations, if he is to produce at all by processes which occupy time.

Keynes then adds the following crucial point:

> These expectations, upon which business decisions depend, fall into two groups, certain individuals or firms being specialised in the business of framing the first type of expectation and others in the business of framing the second. The first type is concerned with the price which a manufacturer can expect to get for his "finished" output at the time when he commits himself to starting the process which will produce it; output being "finished" (from the point of view of the manufacturer) when it is ready to be used or to be sold to a second party. The second type is concerned with what the entrepreneur can hope to earn in the shape of future returns if he purchases (or, perhaps, manufactures) "finished" output as an addition to his capital equipment. We may call the former short-term expectation and the latter long-term expectation.[5]

The two types of expectation are therefore about different things. In the first case, it is the price at which output can be sold which matters. In the second case, it is the more nebulous concept of what can be earned in the shape of "future returns" if there is an addition to capital equipment.

Keynes also describes how the two types of expectation vary in different ways. Short-term expectations, which relate to the cost of output and the sale-proceeds of that output, tend to be revised in a gradual and continuous way, in the light of results as they are realised. Long-term expectations, which relate to an addition to the existing stock of capital equipment (or investment), are, by contrast, subject to sudden revisions: "it is of the nature of long-term expectations that they cannot be checked at short intervals in the light of realised results."[6]

It is relatively easy to fit the ideas of both Knight and Keynes into a Popperian trial and error process. The existence of time brings the element of uncertainty of the future into both production and capital investment, which means that entrepreneurs have no choice but to be guided by their expectations of the future. But whereas it is possible to test expectations for current output by the price mechanism in the short term, so that these kinds of expectation vary in a relatively gradual way, no such possibility exists for the long-term expectations which govern capital investment.

We will look at the problem of long-term expectation and investment in more detail in the next chapter. For the present, it is enough to register the point that, because in the short term expectations can be checked by the price mechanism, such expectations do not usually veer erratically from great over-production to great under-production; or from production boom to production bust. (Conversely, in non-market or command economies, as in those of the Soviet bloc, the absence of a price mechanism did lead to great over-production and under-production.)

A final contribution to the chain of reasoning is provided by Friedrich Hayek. In his 1945 essay entitled "The Use of Knowledge in Society" Hayek describes the price mechanism in a market economy as a system for diffusing knowledge rapidly around society, ensuring that only the most essential information is passed on, and passed on only to those concerned. In a famous metaphor, he wrote of the price system as if it were a kind of machinery for registering change, or:

> a system of telecommunications which enables individual producers to watch merely the movement of a few pointers, as an engineer might watch the hands of a few dials, in order to adjust their activities to changes of which they may never know more than is reflected in the price movement.[7]

The knowledge in society which Hayek is referring to is not knowledge in the sense of scientific theory. Instead, he makes it clear that what he means is useful practical knowledge, of the kind that allows economically productive processes to take place. In fact, he contrasts scientific knowledge with this kind of practical "knowledge of the particular circumstances of time and place". The price mechanism is a social construction, which allows useful knowledge of this nature to be transmitted around society, improving the division of labour.

We can therefore also fit Hayek's approach into the Popperian world view. We have already seen that, according to Popper, knowledge consists not only of scientific theory, but all forms of expectation which are checked by a trial and error process. The price mechanism as described by Hayek is one such method for checking expectations, with the practical knowledge thereby produced allowing individual producers to adjust their activities and output according to the price signals they receive.

Hayek's linkage of the price mechanism with the diffusion of knowledge is therefore not just a manner of speaking. The telecommunications system he describes is indeed a method for increasing useful practical knowledge in an uncertain world, and making possible a better division of labour.

In summary, then, when we put Knight, Keynes and Hayek together we can see there is a substantial body of twentieth century economic thought accepting the idea that the future is open, and subject to genuine uncertainty. Expectations certainly exist, based largely on previous experience, but they are no more than guesses or hypotheses, to be tested through the trial and error process of the price mechanism. This will correct expectations in the short term and allow production to be adjusted to consumption. A market economy allows matters to be brought into balance, and also new things to be brought into being, through an increased division of labour.

So what might disturb this picture?

Anti-competitive behaviour

One thing that clearly can go wrong is if producers short-circuit the price mechanism by agreeing their sales prices to consumers between them, in the form of cartels. In this way they can coordinate their expectations, reduce or eliminate uncertainty between them, and frustrate the operation of the price signalling process.

Since the Second World War, competition policy has developed globally in an attempt to combat this type of behaviour. Policy before then was not always so clear cut, and in the inter-war period views were mixed on whether co-operation between firms might not be better than competition. Immediately after the devastation of the First World War, a wave of international cartels developed in Europe, partly to reduce the frequency and amplitude of price fluctuations and to provide a cushion against prevailing political and economic uncertainty; partly as a result of excess production capacity after the war; and partly to reduce the impact of high rates of inflation and currency volatility. At the League of Nations World Economic Conference in 1927 some delegates argued that cartels might even be a way of increasing international co-operation, which could reduce the scope for conflict.[8]

After the Second World War economic reconstruction was, however, based firmly on competitive principles, encouraged by the influence of US antitrust policy, German ordo-liberal market philosophy and the creation first of the European Coal and Steel Community and then the European common market, both of which included strong competition policy components. Eventually all EU member states have developed domestic competition regimes modelled on EU competition law. The EU as a whole has developed a strong antitrust relationship with the US. And similar competition policies and laws have also been adopted by most developed countries around the world. Although there is no global competition law (an idea which figured in the 1948 International Trade Organisation treaty, but which failed to enter into force after US non-ratification in 1950), there exists a global network of informal co-operation between national competition authorities, with the International Competition Network now numbering over 100 member agencies.

Competition laws vary slightly from jurisdiction to jurisdiction, but nearly always prohibit competing firms from agreeing to fix their sales prices between them, and prohibit firms which occupy a dominant position in any market from abusing that position. Prices in a market are expected to result from a process of free competition between sellers and buyers, which firms should not distort either through agreeing their sales prices between one another, or by unilaterally distorting the market if they are in a position to do so.

In Europe, an impressive body of precedent and case-law has developed in the decades since the 1950s, making clear what is considered to be anti-competitive behaviour by firms operating in the European Economic Area (the vast economic zone comprising the Single Market and the EFTA countries, encompassing over 30 countries with a total population exceeding 500 million). These rules are taken seriously, and large fines are imposed on firms which infringe them, either by the European Commission or by national competition authorities.

The doctrine which has emerged is that competing firms are expected to take their own commercial decisions when putting products on the market, and not coordinate them with other firms. This includes sales prices, but also extends to purchasing decisions and other commercial terms and conditions. The principle is that each firm should exercise its own commercial decision-taking independence on the market.

Competition policy therefore also supports the idea of the price mechanism as a means of testing expectations. The requirement of decision-taking independence means there must be no contacts between competing firms allowing one firm to influence the conduct on the market of another, or to disclose to another its own decisions or intentions on the market. The exchange of information between competing firms will be considered anti-competitive if it removes or reduces the degree of uncertainty as to the operation of the market, with the result that competition between firms is restricted.[9]

In other words, competition policy assumes the existence of uncertainty between firms about the prices they will obtain when selling their products on the market. If that uncertainty is removed, through an agreement or an exchange of information between them, the price mechanism will not function properly. Hayek's telecommunications system cannot be expected to work if firms have private means of communication between them, bypassing it. Knowledge will not be diffused around society, but remain locked up within the firms in question. Expectations of output prices will not be tested.

The open market economy and the open society

As we have seen in this chapter, although it may be new to finance, uncertainty is really no stranger to other parts of the market economy. Since economic processes usually take up time, individuals and firms engaged in production generally have no choice but to rely on expectations of the future when they produce for sale.

18 *Expectations, knowledge and prices*

Adjusting these expectations to what purchasers will pay, through the price mechanism, is a trial and error process, and through it products make their way into the economy and useful knowledge is transmitted around society.

It can be seen there is also a close philosophical link between the ideas of the open market economy and the open society. In both cases the future is open, and not predetermined. Neither the economy nor society as a whole run on pre-set tracks. New things can come into being, and knowledge can increase. However, to preserve this "openness" certain institutions are needed, to ensure checks and balances are maintained, in economic and also political terms. The rule of law, in particular, keeps forces contained that could otherwise dominate and control the economy and society. Popper maintained that the right question in politics should not be, *"Who should rule?"* but rather, *"How can we so organise political institutions that bad or incompetent rulers can be prevented from doing too much damage?"*[10] One might perhaps say something similar in economic life, where the question is not so much, *"Who should produce?"* as, *"How can bad or incompetent producers be prevented from doing too much damage?"*

Although it might appear somewhat unscientific, and rudimentary, the testing of short-term economic expectations through the price mechanism can be compared to the testing of expectations in other forms of existence. If it is only one step from the amoeba to Einstein, the price mechanism is probably rather nearer the former than the latter. But in fact no sophisticated scientific theory is necessary, as long as there can be some practical means of carrying out testing, and expectations can be adjusted in the light of results.

The real problem, as we shall see in the next chapter, is what happens when this is not possible, because economic processes that involve capital investment take up a period of time which extends beyond the short-term operation of the price mechanism, and further out into a more distant and uncertain future.

Notes

1. King M, *The End of Alchemy: Money, Banking and the Future of the Global Economy*, 2016, London, Little, Brown, page 9.
2. Popper K, *All Life is Problem Solving*, 1999, London, Routledge.
3. Popper K, *A World of Propensities*, 1990, Bristol, Thoemmes Press; Popper K and Eccles J, *The Self and Its Brain*, 1977, 1993, London, Routledge; Popper K, *The Open Universe*, 1982, 1995, London, Routledge; Popper K, *Quantum Theory and the Schism in Physics*, 1982, 1989, London, Unwin Hyman.
4. Knight F, *Risk, Uncertainty and Profit*, 1921, Boston, Houghton Mifflin, Part III, Chapter XI, section 8.
5. Keynes, JM, *The General Theory of Employment, Interest and Money*, 1936, London, Macmillan, page 46.
6. *The General Theory of Employment, Interest and Money*, page 51.
7. Hayek F, "The Use of Knowledge in Society", 1945, *American Economic Review*, XXXV, 4: pages 519–530.
8. Gerber D, *Global Competition: Law, Markets and Globalization*, 2010, Oxford, Oxford University Press, page 27.
9. Judgment in Case C-8/08, *T-Mobile Netherlands and Others*, ECR 2009, I-4529, para 35.
10. Popper K, *The Open Society and Its Enemies*, 1971, 1991, London, Routledge, page 121.

3 Beyond price

As a way of testing expectations of the future the price mechanism can only go so far. As we saw in the previous chapter, Keynes classified expectations about the price of current production as "short-term". In practice, relatively few commercial contracts for the sale of products (goods or services) are of more than a few years' duration, at least without a mechanism for the buyer and seller to renegotiate the price. (Exceptions are in areas like energy, where long-term sales contracts offset the high investment costs associated with its production, for example by power stations or through oil extraction.)

Under competition law in Europe, there is a presumption that producers and purchasers should not normally be locked into exclusive arrangements that exceed five years. For the purposes of reviewing competitive markets, competition policy focuses on the actual day-to-day behaviour of producers and purchasers within what are known technically as "relevant markets", a combination of the products in question and the geographical area where they are bought and sold. Companies are considered to be competitors where they are currently active in the same relevant market. A company is considered a *potential* competitor of another if, in response to a permanent price increase in a given relevant market, it is likely to make the additional investments or incur the costs to allow it to enter the market within a short period of time, generally not more than three years.[1]

So today's competition policy focuses on the here and now and the next few years, and output from existing investments. Beyond that, and the further ahead we look into the future, the more uncertain that future becomes. As short-term expectations stretch out into the longer term there becomes less scope for testing expectations against prices. Hayek's telecommunications system may work well when it comes to transmitting signals about prices of current production around the economy, but it is not equipped to foretell the future.

The volatile state of long-term expectations

In the *General Theory* Keynes described what an entrepreneur might earn in the shape of future returns if there is an addition to capital equipment as being subject to "long-term expectation". This type of expectation cannot be checked at short intervals in the light of actual sale results. Nonetheless, it governs the important investment decisions actually taken by companies, which add productive capacity and contribute to future growth.

Collectively, investment decisions taken by individual companies add up to investment in the economy as a whole. It is the erratic flow of investment in the economy as a whole which is the key variable in the Keynesian description of how the economy works. Indeed, it is precisely because there can be sudden and wide fluctuations in this flow of aggregate investment that there is a role in Keynesian economics for public authorities to ensure macroeconomic stability.

Much, therefore, rests upon what determines the state of long-term expectation. The problem, as explained by Keynes in the *General Theory*, is that because of the real difficulty in forecasting an uncertain long-term future, "the daily revaluations of the Stock Exchange, though they are primarily made to facilitate transfers of old investments between one individual and another, inevitably exert a decisive influence on the rate of current investment".

These revaluations of the stocks of existing shares (or old investments), with their "decisive influence" on the rate of current investment, are technically possible because there has developed a separation between the ownership of shares in a company from those who manage it, and the creation of investment markets permitting easy and frequent revaluations of existing investments. (Keynes likens it to a farmer, having tapped his barometer after breakfast, deciding to remove his capital from the farming business between 10 and 11 in the morning, and reconsidering whether he should return to it later in the week.)

So, for companies which have issued shares on the stock market, long-term expectations relating to future capital investment are influenced by the daily revaluations of existing shares, representing old investments. In the absence of any actual trial and error method for testing long-term expectations about investment decisions, this backward looking revaluation of the existing capital stock provides the next best thing, or a proxy pricing system.

But this is an unstable arrangement. There is a famous analysis in the *General Theory* of the many factors affecting the precariousness of these share revaluations on the stock market, with their "decisive influence" on the rate of current investment. One is the decline in knowledge of the underlying business when ownership is dispersed in society. Another is the excessive influence of ephemeral day-to-day fluctuations in profits on share prices. A third is that the market is subject to waves of irrational optimistic and pessimistic sentiment, with a conventional valuation established as the outcome of the "mass psychology of a large number of ignorant individuals" liable to change violently. And a fourth is that professional investors, rather than attempting to correct these tendencies by competing to establish the best long-term forecasts of the probable yields of an investment over its whole life, usually find it easier and more profitable for themselves to attempt to foresee changes in a conventional basis of valuation a short time ahead of the general public, so the question becomes the self-referential one of "anticipating what average opinion expects the average opinion to be".

At this point we could note that an important new concept comes into play when adding to the stock of capital equipment. That is the expected yield of the new capital equipment over its whole life, which may be of many years. This expected yield is not a current price. It is something different – a stream of future income. This stream of income will benefit its owner, so that in the case of a physical capital asset it is the company which makes the investment that benefits. In the case of securities representing shares in companies (or titles to capital assets) it is the holder of the securities. Both are called "investment".

In the *General Theory* a battle takes place between those in the market who attempt to make reasonable estimates of the long-term yield of capital assets (which Keynes calls "enterprise") and those who attempt to forecast the psychology of the investment market (which Keynes calls "speculation"). While the former are more useful to society, Keynes is in little doubt that the latter are more likely to prevail, in particular as investment markets become more organised and liquid (as on Wall Street). It is generally easier and more profitable for intermediaries in the market to attempt to forecast short-term shifts in market sentiment than the long-term streams in income from capital assets. Keynes emphasises here, like Knight, the extreme difficulty of forecasting the future:

> Our knowledge of the factors which will govern the yield of an investment some years hence is usually very slight and often negligible. If we speak frankly, we have to admit that our basis of knowledge for estimating the yield ten years hence of a railway, a copper mine, a textile factory, the goodwill of a patent medicine, an Atlantic liner, a building in the City of London amounts to little and sometimes to nothing; or even five years hence. In fact, those who seriously attempt to make any such estimate are often so much in the minority that their behaviour does not govern the market.

So, in summary, the mechanism set out in the *General Theory* is that long-term expectations, resting upon a fragile basis of knowledge, are unduly influenced by near term observable phenomena, in particular changes in share prices. These shifts in long-term expectations affect investment decisions by individual firms, which collectively translate into investment in the economy as a whole.

The American economist Hyman Minsky incorporated this unstable set-up into his 1986 book *Stabilising an Unstable Economy*. Minsky's own "financial instability hypothesis" rests upon the lack of equilibrium which results from capitalist market mechanisms in the US economy, so that serious business cycles can be caused by the financial attributes of capitalism. According to Minsky, the financing of investment in capital assets, which always contains an element of uncertainty, is a cyclical phenomenon:

> Current views about financing reflect the opinion bankers and businesses hold about the uncertainties they face. These current views reflect the past, and, in particular, the recent past, and how experience is transformed into expectations. A history of success will tend to diminish the margin of safety that business and bankers require and will thus tend to be associated with increased investment; a history of failure will do the opposite.[2]

Is there any modern evidence on this point? According to research published by the Bank for International Settlements in 2016, surveys of the quarterly investment plans of the chief financial officers of large US corporations in the period 1996 to 2012, as well as actual investment undertaken, show that planned and actual investment can be explained by their expectations of earnings growth.[3] These expectations are also highly correlated with the expectations of independent equity analysts, who study the market as a whole. But in both cases, expectations simply extrapolate from the previous year's performance:

> Past-year economic conditions, and both the aggregate and the idiosyncratic component of firm profitability, are all correlated with CFOs' expectational errors. [....] The results [for analysts] are similar: analysts also tend to overestimate next 12-month earnings growth when past-year firm profitability is high and when past-year economic conditions are favourable, and underestimate future earnings growth when the past year is rough.

In other words, faced with the difficulty of forecasting a long-term future, and having to take actual investment decisions covering a period many years ahead, those taking decisions in large US companies tend to extrapolate from economic performance in the recent past.

Minsky, like Keynes, sees the stock market as providing a proxy for the price of capital assets, contributing to the cyclical phenomenon: "A stock market boom leads to a higher implicit market value of the underlying capital assets of the economy; conversely, a fall in the stock market lowers the implicit value."[4] On an aggregate level, the signalling value of stock prices in the US economy has, indeed, been emphasised by none other than the former Chairman of the US Federal Reserve Alan Greenspan: "Stock prices are not merely a leading indicator of business activity but a major contributor to changes in that activity."[5]

Long-term expectations and knowledge

We can now put this long-standing economic problem, identified by Keynes as long ago as the 1930s, into its proper context, with a little help from Popper.

In the face of uncertainty of the future, companies must form the best expectations they can when taking investment decisions, which add to their capital equipment. There is no simple way of testing these expectations, such as by the trial and error process of the price mechanism. The long-term yield of the investment is too far in the future to be able to check expectations of income against it, when the investment decision is taken. Companies therefore tend to fall back on alternative methods, such as to extrapolate from the recent past, and previous experience. The stock price – which is no more than the current view of the market of the value of old investments – helps them do this.

But this is not a reliable trial and error process, as the stock price shifts according to the factors identified by Keynes. In particular, liquid investment markets tend to be dominated not by investors attempting to make reasonable estimates of the long-term yield of capital assets, but by investors attempting to forecast the psychology of the market.

However, once we apply Popper's theory of knowledge, we can see that the activity of forecasting the long-term yield of capital assets ("enterprise") is rather different from the activity of forecasting the psychology of the market ("speculation").

The psychology of the market is affected by many factors which vary over time, and, indeed, change from day to day. Feedback effects occur, particularly at times of crisis and heightened uncertainty, and internal dynamics drown out external signals. It is practically impossible to test these forecasts: the collective psychology (or "sentiment") of the market is always "right", and always adjusts to one event after another. The inability to make repeatable and testable forecasts of these kinds of psychological factors means that attempting to do so is a pseudo-science, akin to astrology and fortune-telling. When Mervyn King describes market prices as being determined by "narratives about fundamentals", rather than fundamentals themselves, he is referring to a similar phenomenon: narratives are like myths – they are plausible shared explanations of perplexing events, not themselves falsifiable. In the terms used by Popper in *The Logic of Scientific Discovery*, they do not have the status of scientific knowledge. They are like metaphysics, or pseudo-science.

By contrast, forecasting the long-term yield of capital assets is, at least in principle, something which is testable and falsifiable. Such a forecast may be correct, or it may be incorrect, but it is possible to test it in the light of experience, or long-term results. Indeed, although long-term investors may be in a minority, Keynes noted in the *General Theory* that they do exist, and "it makes a vast difference to an investment market whether or not [long-term investors] predominate in their influence over the game-players."

Keynes listed a number of different types of capital asset where long-term valuations are in fact easier, because returns in the near future are more certain. The most important class are buildings, where risk can be transferred from the investor to the occupier by means of long-term contracts. Another important class is public utilities, where a substantial proportion of prospective yield is practically guaranteed by monopoly privileges plus the right to charge rates to cover a stipulated margin. (One might, perhaps, add innovations protected by patent to the list.) Keynes also thought that the state, by taking into account the long view and the general social advantage, should be able to do a better job of allocating investment than the fluctuating views of liquid investment markets.

One might develop the point a bit further. Accepting, like Keynes, that there is a very small or negligible basis of knowledge for estimating the yield ten years in the future of any particular capital asset, such as a "railway, a copper mine, a textile factory, the goodwill of a patent medicine, an Atlantic liner, a building in the City of London", the problem might be approached differently. What, for example, have been yields in the past for similar capital assets, or similar classes of capital assets, over earlier ten year periods? Some capital assets will be completely new and unique, and forecasting yields may be a genuine leap in the dark. But other railways, copper mines, Atlantic liners and buildings in the City of London do exist, and it should be possible to base a reasonable estimate – or a reasonable expectation – of yield on experience obtained so far.

The paradox is that, while uncertainty may well hang over each individual capital asset and investment decision, average rates of return on capital appear to be relatively stable. This is a point made by Thomas Piketty in *Capital in the Twenty-First Century*, where he reports that in the period from the eighteenth century to the twenty-first, in both the UK and France the average pure real rate of return on capital (after the costs of management are removed) has oscillated around a central value of 4–5% a year, or more generally in an interval from 3–6% a year: "There has been no pronounced long-term trend either upward or downward."[6] Keynes himself also noticed that in retrospect values are more stable than they appear at the time: "Faced with the perplexities and uncertainties of the modern world, market values will fluctuate much more widely than will seem reasonable in the light of after-events."[7]

So putting these elements together, uncertainty of the longer-term future in this area of economics could be dealt with much like uncertainty elsewhere in science: that is, by creating theories which explain yields and make testable and falsifiable predictions. In this way, and unlike through the pseudo-scientific activity of forecasting the psychology of the market, the stock of knowledge might actually grow.

Theories like this could also be improved as they make predictions about capital assets, and investment in capital assets, so that savings can be allocated more accurately. This would not be alchemy, or magic: merely an application to finance of practices common elsewhere in the social and natural sciences.

In the next chapter we will go on to sketch out what a theoretical approach such as this might resemble.

The way we live now

However, it must be said that the post-Bretton Woods world does not look anything like this at present. As things stand, under the influence of doctrines like the efficient market hypothesis and rational expectations theory, financial prices are assumed to have a meaningful signalling value, just like prices in the real economy. Time is compressed. Hayek's telecommunications system is assumed to work not only to allow producers to take part in the division of labour, but to disseminate useful knowledge around society about long-term investment plans, future risks and global macroeconomic trends.

We can see the consequences of this over-reliance in three areas: stock prices; the extension of bank credit; and currencies.

In the case of stock prices, the dominant theoretical view remains that of the efficient market hypothesis, according to which the prices of securities always reflect all relevant information. As economist Eugene Fama put it in the introduction to his 1970 paper "Efficient Capital Markets: A Review of Theory and Empirical Work", the primary role of the capital market is to allocate ownership of the capital stock of the economy, and the ideal is a market in which prices provide accurate signals for resource allocation. This is, in other words:

> a market in which firms can make production-investment decisions, and investors can choose among the securities that represent ownership of the firms' activities under the assumption that securities prices at any time 'fully reflect' all available information. A market in which prices always 'fully reflect' available information is called 'efficient'.[8]

A corollary of this hypothesis is that the more trading there is in the market the more price signals will be created (through a process of what is sometimes called "price discovery"), which will benefit both firms and investors.

While this is the economic justification for the very high volumes of trading in securities which have developed in the post-Bretton Woods world, it is completely at odds with Keynes' view of investment markets, as described above. The risk he foresaw is that, rather than becoming more efficient, the bigger and more developed an investment market becomes, the more forecasting the psychology of the market (or speculation) will come to dominate it.

In today's investment markets, a high proportion of activity is, indeed, speculation (in the sense of the word used by Keynes). The average holding period of US shares was around four years at the end of the Second World War, but had fallen to around eight months by 2000 and around two months by 2008.[9] This means that a high proportion of shares are bought, not because of their prospective long-term yield, but because a favourable change is expected in their market value. This is the textbook definition of speculation (if by textbook we mean the *General Theory*). Trading volumes have, in the meantime, increased enormously, from about 2 million shares per day in the 1950s to 8.5 billion per day in recent years – 4,250 times as many.[10]

As stock prices reflect the short-term expectations of investors, each attempting to anticipate the short-term reactions of others, they lose their usefulness as proxy prices for new investment by the firms who have issued the stock. In the quotation from Fama, above, an efficient market is said to be one where firms can base "production-investment" decisions on securities prices. But this does not happen. Production decisions by firms are not, in fact, based on stock prices at all, but rather on expectations of sales in the relatively short term. By contrast, investment decisions by firms may well be based on securities prices, but the more they are subject to short-term speculative movements the less reliable a guide they are to the long-term future.

Aggregate levels of business investment in both the US and the UK have been declining in recent decades (despite this huge growth in trading activity). The explanation of economist Andrew Smithers is that those approving investment decisions in companies are more concerned with maintaining their immediate share price (in particular through share buy-backs) than investing for future long-term growth. The reason for this is that their own personal remuneration is linked to the share price, via bonus schemes like stock options. The consequence is a focus on the short term rather than the long term, reduced investment and therefore reduced economic growth: "So long as the present system lasts, we will have a level of investment that is inadequate to meet the current hopes and expectations for growth."[11]

(Another, less Machiavellian, explanation may simply be that the speculative nature of stock prices provides signals for companies which are hard to translate into long-term investment decisions.)

The extension of credit by banks has also become dangerous in the post-Bretton Woods world when sight has been lost of reasonable estimates of the underlying yields of capital assets against which credit is extended (in most cases property, or real estate), and banks over-lend in anticipation of price appreciation. If a sufficient number of banks do this collectively, asset prices will be buoyed upward until the supply of credit diminishes, or ceases, at which point they will collapse. There have been several major international credit bubbles and crashes caused in this way since the 1970s, and many lesser episodes. The price signals from rising property values have come to displace long-term yields. Even though buildings fall into a class of capital assets where, as Keynes noted, it should be possible to offset uncertainty by means of long-term tenancy agreements, this has not happened and short-term prices provide an insufficient guide to the long-term future.

In the case of currencies, since the end of the Bretton Woods system (when values of currencies were fixed to the dollar, and the value of the dollar fixed to gold) there has been a global regime of floating rates, only loosely connected to the real economy. Currencies are traded mostly on the huge inter-bank foreign exchange market, and most trading in currencies is not related to the needs of real economy international businesses or individuals, but to speculation (in the Keynesian sense) in this inter-bank market.

How do expectations affect currency markets? A good analysis can be found in a 1983 paper by former US Federal Reserve and Treasury official Robert Roosa, who experienced both the Bretton Woods system until 1971 and after that today's regime of floating rates. After observing that international movements in capital flows do not conform to standard economic theory as developed for trade in real economy goods and services, Roosa suggested the following combination of factors is responsible for the bulk of trading from one currency to another in the foreign exchange markets.

First, because interest rates differ among differing leading global economies (reflecting differing domestic economic circumstances), and currencies in offshore markets closely mirror domestic rates for the same currency, holders of funds engaging in international transactions are drawn to currencies offering the higher real interest rates, provided they do not see offsetting foreign exchange risks.

Second, as interest rates attract funds towards some currencies and away from others, those needing currencies for use in making future payments attempt to minimise risks of exchange rate loss by anticipating future movements. The consequence of attempts to avoid exchange losses is a bandwagon effect, as under the influence of rapid shifts of funds strong currencies become stronger and weak currencies weaker.

Third, in a world of continuously varying political uncertainty, repeated instances arise where holders of funds become fearful as to the future prospects of a particular economy, whether for internal or external reasons. The result is a run into other currencies that appear less vulnerable to such risks. "And the sea of fluid currencies available for making such runs is so large that the resulting exchange rate changes can appear as tidal waves."[12]

It is, therefore, shifting expectations about the future worth of various currencies which drive currency movements. Because these expectations are not rooted in any trial and error method connected to the real economy, whereby they can be checked easily, they can veer erratically, magnifying short-term price signals. The consequences for currencies were well described by hedge fund operator George Soros, writing a few years after Roosa:

> [S]peculative capital is motivated primarily by expectations about future exchange rates. To the extent that exchange rates are dominated by speculative capital transfers, they are purely reflexive: expectations relate to expectations and the prevailing bias can validate itself almost indefinitely. The situation is highly unstable: if the opposite bias prevailed it could also validate itself. The greater the relative importance of speculation, the more unstable the system becomes: the total rate of return can flip-flop with every change in the prevailing bias.[13]

Soros himself has developed a theory of "reflexivity", under which, as in the example of currencies, expectations feed off expectations and create collective biases, mistakes and feedback effects. We will look at this in more detail in the next chapter, but the point could be made here that these phenomena are explicable in the absence of a simple trial and error method for testing expectations, and an over-reliance on short-term price signals.

To the examples of stock prices, credit and currencies might be added commodities, the building blocks of the world economy, also increasingly traded in short-term speculative markets in recent years, and also become unstable. The problem in all these cases is that in the face of long-term uncertainty (a permanent feature of nearly all such markets), short-term price movements become a fluctuating and erratic influence on, and guide to, long-term expectations.

It is as if not only the farmers of the world, but the builders, the manufacturers, the butchers, the bakers and the candlestick makers and all those who supply them and engage in world commerce have to make their plans and move their capital in and out of their business, relying on shifting signals emitted from day to day by a temperamental and hyperactive barometer.

Beyond price

If the price system is an unreliable guide to the long-term future what is the alternative? We need to examine a little more closely the concept of yield, introduced earlier in connection with investment in capital assets.

Yield is not a price (although rights to yields, in the form of securities, can be bought and sold for a price). Yield is the long-term stream of income which flows from the creation of a new capital asset, which is capital investment by a company. It is also the long-term stream of income which flows from owning securities, such as shares in companies.

"Investment", confusingly, therefore means two completely different activities: the physical creation of a new capital asset by a company (or the collective creation of new assets in the economy as a whole); and also the allocation of savings, by individuals or pools of savings in funds, to company shares. The latter is a purely financial activity, not connected at all to physical investment by a company in new capital assets. There is also a difference in time sequence. Investment in the financial sense nearly always means buying from the stock of existing shares, already issued in the market and held by other investors. Investment in the physical sense, on the other hand, means the creation of a new capital asset, which did not exist before.

To pay for new physical investment, a company generally has three choices: to use its own funds from retained profits arising from previous business activities; to obtain additional loan or credit financing, whether from a bank or by issuing bonds; or to issue shares on the capital market, bringing in additional equity finance. In practice, as observed by the economist John Kay, large companies have not been using either the London or New York stock exchanges to raise funds to expand their businesses in any significant way at all in recent years. Instead, self-financing is the rule today, using cash from a company's own operations.[14] In other words, there is today hardly any direct relationship at all between the financing of new physical investment and the ownership of shares in a company. And there is today only the most tenuous connection between aggregate savings and aggregate investment in new capital assets by companies.

We will look at this problem further in the next chapter, but first a word on how yield is calculated.

In the *General Theory*, Keynes described the prospective yield of a capital asset as being like a series of annuities, which the owner expects to obtain from selling its output, after deducting the running expenses of obtaining that output, during the life of the asset. This prospective yield is one factor, to be added to a second factor, the supply price of the capital asset, with together make up the marginal efficiency of capital, which determines whether investment actually takes place. But unlike the supply price of a capital asset, which *is* a current price, prospective yield is based upon expectations. It is not static, and it is not merely the current yield. Expectations of prospective yield are based partly upon existing known facts, like the existing stock of capital assets, and demand for its output; and partly upon future events, about which forecasts can be made with greater or lesser confidence. This state of confidence in turn is affected by the shifting state of the stock market, revaluing old investments (as noted, above). Prospective yield therefore is a complex mechanism, with fixed and moving parts.

Modern methods of investment appraisal by companies range from simple "payback" calculations for some investment projects to complicated calculations of internal rates of return and net present value for larger more complicated projects. However, more sophisticated methods of investment appraisal invariably run into the problem of comparing the cost of carrying out projects with returns from the stock market, as in Keynes. These, then, rest upon the modern assumption that the stock market is "efficient", in the sense described by Fama, above. As pointed out in a standard textbook on the subject: "in an inefficient stock market, it would be virtually impossible for managers to take rational capital investment decisions on behalf of the company's shareholders."[15]

Whichever method is chosen, it is clear that the concept of yield is very different from the concept of a price. Yield is connected to what Knight called "the forward-looking character of the economic process itself". By its very nature, it reaches into an uncertain future, whereas a price is a current, known quantity. A series of prices resulting from transactions throughout a ten-year period, from trading between investors in titles to capital assets in the form of securities, is not the same thing as the actual yield of that same investment over that ten-year period. A series of short terms does not equate to a long term.

On the other hand, although yield reaches into an uncertain future it is not a completely unknown quantity. It is possible to make reasonable estimates of yield, and while at any one moment the market price of a capital asset might be volatile, long-term returns are usually on average relatively stable.

A final comment might be made on the difference between real economy prices and financial prices. With real economy prices, for goods and services, a better division of labour is usually created by transactions within a market, so that producers and purchasers can be brought together and the economy can grow. But financial prices resulting from transactions in liquid investment markets are not bringing producers and purchasers together, and nothing new is being produced. All that is happening is that titles to existing capital assets are being exchanged. Prices might vary dramatically, but the underlying capital stock stays the same. No matter how much trading takes place, the economy does not grow.

Recapitulation

Before we go further, it may be helpful to summarise the content of this chapter. Unlike short-term expectations, the long-term expectations of companies relating to investments in new capital assets cannot easily be checked by a trial and error method against actual sales results, through the price mechanism. Instead, in the face of an uncertain long-term future, expectations tend to be based on previous experience, an extrapolation of the recent past and the stock price. But stock prices in liquid markets are dominated by those attempting to forecast the psychology of the market, in itself a pseudo-science, incapable of testing and falsification. This method is an unreliable guide to the future.

By contrast, expectations of streams of income (yields) from new capital assets could be placed on a more solid footing by the use of theories which are testable and falsifiable, in the light of experience. This is the normal way in which uncertainty of the future is dealt with in science. It is the absence of such a method which causes excessive reliance to be placed on stock prices, which do no more than revalue old capital assets. Matters could be improved. Astrology might become astronomy.

Notes

1. European Commission, *Guidelines on the applicability of Article 101 of the Treaty on the Functioning of the European Union to Horizontal Cooperation Agreements*, 2011, OJEU C11, 14.1.2011, para 10.
2. Minsky H, *Stabilising an Unstable Economy*, 1986, 2008, New York, McGraw Hill, page 209.
3. Gennaioli N, Ma Y and Shleifer A, "Expectations and Investment", 2016, *Bank for International Settlements Working Paper 562*.
4. *Stabilising an Unstable Economy*, page 208.
5. Greenspan A, *The Map and the Territory*, 2013, London, Allen Lane, page 80.
6. Piketty T, *Capital in the Twenty-First Century*, 2014, Cambridge, Massachusetts, Belknap, page 206.
7. Speech to the National Mutual Life Assurance Society, 1938, London.
8. Fama E, "Efficient Capital Markets: A Review of Theory and Empirical Work", 1970, *Journal of Finance*, 25, 2: pages 383–417.
9. Haldane A, "The Race to Zero", 2011, speech, Bank of England.
10. Bogle J, *The Clash of the Cultures*, 2012, Hoboken, New Jersey, John Wiley and Sons, page 3.
11. Smithers A, *The Road to Recovery*, 2013, Chichester, John Wiley and Sons, page 227.
12. Roosa R, "Economic Instability and Flexible Exchange Rates", *World Money and National Policies* (papers by Wallich H, Emminger O, Kenen P and Roosa R), 1983, New York, Group of Thirty.
13. Soros G, *The Alchemy of Finance*, 1987, 1994, New York, John Wiley and Sons, page 74.
14. Kay J, *Other People's Money*, 2015, London, Profile Books, page 161.
15. Lumby S, *Investment Appraisal and Financial Decisions*, 1981, 1994, London, Chapman and Hall, page 366.

4 Savings, investment and liquidity

This chapter will outline how a workable and falsifiable theory of finance might be approached. Before doing so, we need briefly to remind ourselves of the current state of the investment industry; to consider an alternative theory of "reflexivity" in financial markets, as developed by George Soros; and also to look at the issue of "liquidity".

The outstanding shift in the post-war period has been towards institutionalised savings and investment. Rather than individuals running companies or making personal investment decisions in companies using their own savings, company ownership through shares is today dispersed widely around society, and individual savings are pooled into collective savings, like pension funds, insurance funds and mutual funds. It is these collective savings, in the form of funds, which today carry out most financial investment, and are responsible for the ownership of shares in companies.

There has been an apparently inexorable rise in pooled and managed savings, from an estimated global US$11 trillion in 1990 to US$87 trillion in 2014 and a projected US$100 trillion by 2020.[1] The economist Hyman Minsky described this trend in 1996, "in which the proximate owners of a vast proportion of financial instruments are mutual and pension funds", as "money manager capitalism".[2]

It might, perhaps, have been thought that this growth of institutional and professional investment would naturally lead to a more long-term and professional analysis of the underlying values of companies, so that "enterprise" (making reasonable estimates of the long-term yield of capital assets) would come to displace "speculation" (attempting to forecast the psychology of the market).

In his engaging account of the origins and development of the US investment industry, John Bogle (founder of the US firm Vanguard, today the world's largest mutual fund), describes, somewhat ruefully, how he expected exactly that in the 1950s, at the dawn of the US mutual fund industry. Instead, the opposite happened: over the ensuing six decades institutional investors, just like the professional investors described in Keynes' *General Theory* in the 1930s, continued to be drawn into short-term speculation. Trading volumes and turnovers of stock increased massively, and holding periods shortened. Bogle calculates that, compared to an average US$250 billion a year of new capital brought to US companies through the stock market (via initial public offerings and secondary offerings), average annual stock trading by 2011 reached a volume of US$33 trillion – over 100 times more.[3]

Moreover, as Bogle also points out, there is an important difference between the short-term price movements of the stocks of individual companies and longer-term trends, which are much more stable. Thus, in the previous 150 years to 2012, Bogle records that a combination of dividend yields and real, after-inflation earnings growth of US companies have aggregated at about 7% annually (4.5% yield, 2.5% real earnings growth), which is almost exactly the same as the real return of 7% in stock prices.[4] However, at any one time, stock prices, through speculation in the market, can easily diverge widely from the underlying long-term trend. In Bogle's words: "*investors are more volatile than investments*".

Why is this? Bogle (like others) sees the problem as essentially a principal/agent one. Institutional investors, rather than focusing on the long-run stable returns which their principals (end savers) require, focus instead on the opportunities for short-term speculative price appreciation which can enrich them as agents (being, as they invariably are in a system of institutionalised investment, profit-maximising firms in their own right). Thus, mutual funds, which by 2011 had become the largest holder of US stocks (with a 30% market share), have been turning over their portfolio at an average of 100% a year since 1985.

At the London School of Economics, Paul Woolley and colleagues have gone a step further, and use the principal/agent relationship to explain how financial markets have come to depart from the equilibrium implied by the efficient market hypothesis. Financial institutions and funds (as agents) are in particular prone to "momentum" (short-term, speculative) trading, despite the fact this is against the interests of end savers, as principals. And it is the large flows of finance between these funds which then perpetuate momentum price effects, with the resulting mispricing of financial assets, and inefficient markets. Any targets or benchmarks based on the inaccurate prices formed in these inefficient markets will be inaccurate, as will any derivative instruments based on them. The solution Woolley and colleagues suggest is for principals (end savers) to exercise much greater control over their agents (financial institutions), to ensure they take the longer term view, in the best interests of the principals.

We will include these insights when we look at a falsifiable theory of finance, below.

A first approximation: the theory of reflexivity

The vast scale of the sums involved in today's institutionalised finance, very little of which is connected to long-term investment, provides the backdrop for an understanding of George Soros's own theory of reflexivity, mentioned in the previous chapter. Since Soros himself has been greatly influenced by the philosopher Karl Popper, his viewpoint deserves consideration.

The argument of Soros is that financial markets provide an extreme, but vivid, example of a general social phenomenon. In the face of imperfect knowledge of the future (which he takes from Popper) mistaken expectations can be built up between market participants which, when they are shared, may not be properly corrected but rather become mutually reinforcing, eventually parting company from reality, sometimes with disastrous consequences when the mistake becomes obvious to everyone (causing a sharp price correction). This reflexive process can be used to explain boom–bust processes in financial markets, but Soros take it further: reflexive processes can be found generally in society, such as in post-modern methods of thinking where perceptions of reality can be manipulated by opinion-shapers and political strategists and leaders, but prove to become reality, in a form of self-fulfilling prophecy.

Soros suggests this phenomenon is, however, most clearly seen in finance:

> Nowhere is the role of expectations more clearly visible than in financial markets. Buy and sell decisions are based on expectations about future prices, and future prices, in turn, are contingent on present buy and sell decisions. To speak of supply and demand as if they were determined by forces that are independent of the market participants' expectations is quite misleading.[5]

It should be noted that, while Soros is very much inspired by Popper, he does depart from him on one important point. Unlike Popper, Soros holds there is no "unity of scientific method", because the methods and criteria applicable to the natural sciences do not apply to the social sciences, including politics and economics (and financial economics). Soros holds there is a fundamental difference between the two, because social sciences, unlike natural sciences, have to deal with events that have thinking participants. It is precisely because these thinking participants base their decisions on their imperfect understanding that reflexive feedback mechanisms can be set up, leading to distorting consequences in the social sciences, including finance.

This approach leads Soros on to the idea that both politics and economics can veer from being in "equilibrium" to being "far from equilibrium". Being in equilibrium means, essentially, that the erroneous expectations arising from imperfect knowledge of the future cancel each other out, so no one tendency becomes dominant. Far from equilibrium situations can occur in politics (he cites crises of European totalitarianism), and also in finance, if the unchecked errors of expectations are shared too widely, and allowed to accumulate to disastrous proportions, until the inevitable crash occurs.

There is much in what Soros says about the role of expectations in finance which appears correct, and it must be said that Soros has been spectacularly successful over the decades as a hedge fund operator in financial markets, which suggests that in these markets he is much better at reading developments and foreseeing their impact than other operators. But ultimately he goes too far, or overstates his case. Why is this?

Soros argues as if financial markets represented a simple extension of other forms of economic activity, and that stock markets, foreign exchange markets, banking and all forms of credit (or, as he puts it, "all financial markets that serve as a discounting mechanism for future developments") are the same as markets in the real economy which process normal goods and services.

But this brings us back to the distinction between real economy market prices and financial market prices we have seen in earlier chapters. Short-term expectations in real economy markets for normal goods and services may be corrected by the operation of the price mechanism, bringing buyers (customers) and sellers (producers) together. But financial markets, serving as "a discounting mechanism for future developments", are doing something different: in a two-price system market economy they are valuing future income flows from outstanding financial and capital assets.

While accepting that much of what Soros says about the deficiencies and disequilibria of modern financial markets is correct and perceptive, it may on the whole be simpler to look for the explanation in the operations and institutions of the financial markets which create problems of expectation, rather than seeking the answer in the nature of consciousness, or the role of thinking participants in shaping reality.

Nor need we take the drastic step of abandoning the unity of scientific method, and view the social sciences (including financial economics) as different from the natural sciences. As we saw in earlier chapters, Popper's theory of knowledge already includes a role for thinking participants, and indeed rests upon the existence of prior expectations – some based on direct experience, some inborn and unconscious – which can be tested by a trial and error process. Popper certainly accepts, like Soros, that individuals have an imperfect understanding of the future, and are highly fallible, but that is no reason to abandon the search for better objective knowledge, through the development of better scientific theories. If social sciences abandon the search for falsifiable theories they would be doomed to remain pseudo-sciences, which rest upon myths and stories about perplexing events that can never be tested. (Soros may recognise this when he entitled one of this books *The Alchemy of Finance*.)

If we adopt Popper's critical scientific method, the financial markets which Soros identifies might be considered as man-made institutions, with structures that can easily be analysed, tested and improved. In the case of stock markets, the possibility they are unstable and can boom and crash was evident as long ago as the *General Theory* of 1936, with the memory of the crash of 1929 still fresh. In the post-war period organised investment markets have grown much larger, and a new layer of professional money managers has interposed itself, handling collective savings. But the underlying instability has not been cured.

Today's foreign exchange markets are almost entirely a creation of the post-Bretton Woods period. Turnover today far exceeds that of stock markets, and is almost entirely on the inter-bank market, where one bank buys and sells foreign exchange to another. Relatively little supply and demand for foreign exchange comes from real economy firms or individuals trading goods and services internationally: the bulk is from banks themselves, driven by fluctuating expectations of the relative values of currencies.

Banking and credit also depend upon an institutional framework, encompassing the relationship between the central bank and commercial banks, the protection of depositors, the official rate of interest, the effectiveness of bank regulation, and so forth. Once again, the possibility that banks can be unstable should be no surprise: on one authoritative count there have been no fewer than 40 banking crises in the world's most developed financial centres since 1800 (in the UK, the US and France).[6] That banking crises have become larger and more international in the post-war period (or more particularly in the more liberal post-Bretton Woods period) may simply reflect the globalisation of an underlying instability.

In short, the aberrant characteristics in these financial markets, which Soros rightly pinpoints, may be rather more easily explained by features, structures and institutions of the markets themselves, than by abandoning the unity of scientific method.

The uses and abuses of liquidity

Before going on to outline an alternative theoretical approach to this problem, a further concept does need introducing into the picture, which is that of liquidity.

"Liquidity" in today's financial markets means the ability to buy and sell financial assets without a transaction having an effect on the overall market price. For that reason, it is usually assumed that high levels of liquidity are a good thing, and indeed the more liquidity there is the better (and therefore the more trading of financial assets the better). Conversely, low levels of liquidity, making it impossible to buy or sell assets without an impact on a market price, are assumed to be undesirable. If, for example, it is impossible to sell assets, because they are illiquid, prices are likely to drop in a fire sale. For that reason, banks are required to hold a proportion of their assets in a form which is liquid, or easily saleable.

Although it is widely believed today that liquidity is a good thing, and even an end in itself, there is an alternative view. This is that while liquidity may be desirable from the point of view of an individual, or a financial institution, this does not hold true for the economy as a whole. In the *General Theory* Keynes took a cautious view of liquidity, developing a theory of "liquidity-preference" to describe the circumstances under which individuals and firms will prefer to hold savings in unproductive liquid money form (cash or near-cash). Because money in cash or near-cash form provides no interest to its holder, holding assets in this way only makes sense in the face of uncertainty about holding assets in other forms, which would provide long-term yields. Keynes worked out his theory most completely in terms of bonds, since if the future rate of interest is known it is more advantageous to purchase interest-bearing bonds than to hold non-interest-bearing cash as a store of wealth. "Liquidity-preference" is therefore closely related to his view of the role of uncertainty in the economy.

Keynes was also critical of the role of organised liquid investment markets, whether for the purchase of securities in capital assets (the stock market), or for the purchase of debts (the bond market), since as such markets develop the scope for speculation on them increases. He saw a genuine dilemma: it is only because there are such liquid markets, permitting investment commitments to be revised, that otherwise unproductively hoarded savings might be drawn on and used for investment. On the other hand, as these markets develop, speculation increases, rendering long-term investment more difficult. In an uncertain world the only radical solution to this dilemma would be for an individual to have no choice between consuming his income and ordering the production of the specific capital asset which seems the most promising investment available:

> It might be that, at times when he was more than usually assailed by doubts concerning the future, he would turn in his perplexity towards more consumption and less new investment. But that would avoid the disastrous, cumulative and far-reaching repercussions of its being open to him, when thus assailed by doubts, to spend his income neither on the one nor on the other.[7]

The post-war advent of institutionalised savings and investment (or "money manager capitalism") is a major new factor here. It might be thought that money managers, on behalf of savers, should really require less liquidity, because they are dealing with savings already committed to investment. (These savings are not being hoarded, in other words.) They should, therefore, be able to devote a higher proportion of pooled savings to long-term investment. But in practice, as investment markets have expanded, the scope for short-term speculation has also increased, and today's collective savings are, to a very large extent, devoted to trading between money managers, exchanging titles to existing capital assets in the hope of a favourable change in market value.

The wider macroeconomic problem here is that the pooled savings which are accumulating (today equivalent to something like total world GDP) are being withdrawn from present consumption, and not being used for new investment, creating future growth. This means they are not adding to but rather subtracting from effective demand in the world's economy ("effective demand" being the sum of consumption plus investment). The consequences, in the words used by Keynes, may indeed be "disastrous, cumulative and far-reaching."

Is there a better way forward?

Out of alchemy: towards a better theory of finance

It is now time to put all these various elements together and attempt to sketch out a possible approach to a workable theory of finance. ("Theory" here means a testable and falsifiable explanation of phenomena, which is certainly not meant to be definitive, and can be improved on and contribute to the growth of knowledge.)

The starting point for any such theory is a recognition that the future is open and uncertain. This is always the case. In this respect the world of economics and finance is no different from any other social or natural science. But in the short term in the normal, real economy, where products (goods and services) are exchanged, the trial and error method of the price mechanism can act as an effective test of expectations of the future. No theory is called for.

The longer-term future, relevant to adding to the stock of capital equipment (or new investment), is different because it is subject to greater uncertainty. Current prices are not a reliable test of long-term expectations. Something more is needed, which can help predict yields (future streams of income from capital assets). While it is always difficult to be precise in specific circumstances, the yields of new capital assets are not, however, completely arbitrary, or unknown. Average rates of return on capital prove to be surprisingly stable. Previous yields obtained on comparable capital assets can also be established. Moreover, when we move to the level of entire companies, returns to investors may be volatile in the short term but also turn out to be relatively stable in the long term, where it is known, for example, that the real economic value of US companies progresses broadly in line with the growth in GDP. For the larger established companies, records can also be found of long-term performance (measured in terms of dividend yield and earnings growth) over periods of many years in the past; in some cases periods of many decades.

When we turn then to the side of savers and investors, most investment these days is through the medium of professionally-managed pooled funds, on behalf of individual end savers (pension funds, insurance schemes, mutual funds, etc.). Although this extra layer of intermediaries could in theory provide more professionalism and expertise, in practice it has become beset by principal/agent problems and the short-termism identified by Keynes in the 1930s. Hardly any of this collective saving is used for new investment (i.e. the creation of new capital assets). Most is devoted to the short-term buying and selling of titles to already existing capital assets, in liquid investment markets.

However, as the research at the London School of Economics indicates, the longer term the liabilities of these funds, the worse a focus on the short term is for their end savers. Investors and funds (like hedge funds) with purely short-term time horizons can (perhaps) afford to focus on short-term price movements, where the essential question is timing market trends ("speculation" in the sense meant by Keynes). But over the long term this kind of short-term behaviour erodes the value of the larger funds, because they must continue over this long period of time to be successful at timing market movements and incur transaction costs, while being constrained by practices like index benchmarking, making them predictable and vulnerable to short-term predatory behaviour by their competitors. As trenchantly pointed out by Woolley: "Pension funds are having their assets exchanged with other pension funds at a rate of 25 times in the life of the average liability for no collective advantage but at a cost that reduces the end-value of the pension by around 30%".[8] For larger funds with long-term liabilities and horizons, a focus on the underlying cash flows and streams of income from owning financial assets is in fact a better and more productive strategy. In the terminology of Keynes, this is based on making "reasonable estimates of the long-term yield of capital assets" (or "enterprise").

There is, then, when we put them together, a curious symmetry in the two worlds of finance and the real economy. In the short term prices have a signalling value, but over the longer term prices lose their usefulness and yields take over. In the real economy, the short-term time horizon depends on the nature of the production process, when prices are set between producers and purchasers. In finance, the short-term time horizon depends more on the relevant profit period of those managing the money, which may not be the same as the actual long-term obligations or liabilities of funds – creating a principal/agent problem. The essential theoretical question becomes then one of meshing yields in the two worlds of finance and the real economy.

To bring the two sides together, and allow a better match of savings with investment, data could be assembled of actual historic yields obtained from existing capital assets and companies, to allow a first approximation to be made of likely future yields from these (or similar) capital assets and companies. This historic data would then provide a reasonable basis for making investments based on these estimates. The future is, as always, uncertain, but, as in any other branch of science, reasonable estimates based on previous experience can still be made.

Moreover, such estimates can then in due course be checked against the actual yields obtained, as time goes by, through a process of trial and error. In this way, the estimating process can be improved and refined, and expectations corrected. As this process continues, the volumes of savings devoted to particular types of investment might also be adjusted, in the light of experience. Long-term returns based on yield could then be matched with increasing accuracy with the liabilities of savings funds.

A falsifiable theory would thus be built up, providing explanations of yields from various types of capital assets and companies, whether there is a propensity for mean values to assert themselves under certain circumstances (in average, or over long periods of time), what might constitute exceptional circumstances, and so forth.

As more stable pools of long-term savings develop, companies should be able to draw on them to fund their own new investment projects (the creation of new capital assets). This, then, would add to retained earnings and bank finance as a further and more stable source of new investment funding.

This kind of procedure, whereby estimates are made which can be checked against results (which are then fed back into the forecasting process, which thereby improves) is comparable to procedures adopted elsewhere in other branches of science. In today's climate science, for example, highly complex models are created which permit projections of atmospheric shifts. Models are evaluated which incorporate data from huge numbers of sources, and continue to be refreshed as new data comes in. Given that the future is always uncertain, any given projection may of course be incorrect, but the interaction of better models, using enormous computing power, and more reassessed data means that climate science is improving, and knowledge is increasing.

As Popper put it, more generally:

> The natural as well as the social sciences always start from problems, from the fact that something inspires amazement in us, as the Greek philosophers used to say. To solve these problems, the sciences use fundamentally the same method that common sense employs, the method of trial and error. To be

more precise, it is the method of trying out solutions to our problem and then discarding the false ones as erroneous. This method assumes that we work with a large number of experimental solutions. One solution after another is put to the test and eliminated.[9]

Implications

What would it mean to have a workable and falsifiable theory of finance, along the lines described above?

First, a number of structural deficiencies in financial markets begin to look soluble. Boom and bust processes appear to arise when all sight is lost of underlying yield, and collective over-optimistic (or over-pessimistic) expectations of price changes take hold of market participants in liquid markets. An anchoring of expectations in yields, which are much more stable, should have a stabilising effect generally.

Second, a better rate of return from collective savings like pension funds might be envisaged. Since, as Woolley points out, end values of pension funds can be eaten up dramatically by the costs of collectively self-defeating transactions – to the tune of almost a third – pension returns should be capable of significant improvement. Moreover, since the benefits of long-term investment are indeed long term, increased longevity should become affordable and pension deficits reduce. Pension funds could become a source of economic strength, not crises and reducing returns.

Third, the tenuous and almost non-existent connection between physical and financial investment might be improved. The volumes of pooled and managed savings now accumulating are, as we have seen, on a macroeconomically significant scale. The estimated US$87 trillion accumulated globally by 2014 is roughly equivalent to the size of world GDP. If sums of this magnitude are not being used for present day consumption, and not being used for new physical investment, they are a drag on demand in the world economy, no doubt contributing to the mediocre and imbalanced growth seen in recent decades. (By way of comparison, total EU consumption in 2008, representing about 57% of EU GDP, only came to about EUR 6.6 trillion (US$8.6 trillion): total EU investment, representing about 21% of EU GDP, came to about EUR 2.4 trillion (US$3.1 trillion).)[10]

If we compare these figures with actual physical investment by real companies we can also see the difference. US$87 trillion in institutional savings is over 4,000 times the actual 2013 investment expenditure of US$20 billion by Exxon Mobil, the world's largest private investor and a significant fraction of all US investment – and entirely financed from internal company resources.[11] Even a slight increase, of the order of a few percentage points, in the proportion of savings making its way into new investment should have major economic benefits.

A workable theory of finance such as this might also allow a new type of capital market to be envisaged. More details on how this might be done are contained in Chapter Eight.

Is there a passive alternative?

One practical response to the evident deficiencies and costs of institutionalised investment has been the shift in recent years to completely "passive" forms of investment, which make no pretence to select individual company stocks, or to time short-term price movements. Instead, in its simplest form (pioneered by US mutual fund Vanguard in 1976), passive investment merely tracks an index of the entire US stock market, such as the Standard & Poor's 500 index. Moreover, the kind of mutual fund espoused by Vanguard truly is mutual (in the sense that it is owned by its investors), so principal/agent problems seen elsewhere in the industry can be reduced, or even eliminated.

From small beginnings, this style of investment fund has grown to be very popular, by 2012 totalling US$2.4 trillion, accounting for more than a quarter of all US equity fund assets.[12] Vanguard itself has become the world's largest mutual fund. Rather than engaging in costly short-term market-timing, or "speculation" (in the Keynesian sense), costs are reduced to the bare minimum by merely keeping the fund aligned on the performance of the stock market as a whole, irrespective of the relative performance of individual companies within it. Individual savers can deposit or withdraw funds, but the object of the fund as a whole is to be permanently based on the entire stock market.

John Bogle, the founder of Vanguard, has explained the logic behind it in terms similar to the analysis of Keynes in the *General Theory*. Since individual stock prices are subject to speculative movements it makes no sense for an investment fund to attempt to keep track of them. Instead, all that is required is to keep track of an aggregate figure, represented by an index, which has become possible since the 1970s through the development of computing power. And, as Bogle has also pointed out, since there is a disjunction between short-term price movements of the stocks of individual companies and longer-term trends, which are much more stable, the longer the time-frame for investment, the better.

Passive investment on these lines appears, then, to be a reasonable practical response to the short-termism in the markets resulting from "money manager capitalism". It sidesteps the difficulty of timing market movements by following an aggregate index representing the market as a whole. And it uses the innovation of computing power to allow the fund to adopt a long-term position, in a way Keynes would not himself have foreseen.

Despite these advantages, there may be drawbacks. One is that a stock market index itself can easily also become the subject of short-term trading, or speculation. Thus, in the US since the 1990s there have developed exchange traded funds (ETFs) based on various forms of indices, including the Standard & Poor's 500 index. By 2013 the most actively traded security in the US was an ETF based on this very index, known as the SPDR S & P 500 ETF, launched in 1993. ETFs have proliferated in all directions, based on indices related to the stock market as a whole; on various segments of the stock market (like technology stocks); on international stock markets; on commodities; on bonds; and on currencies. The creation of an index therefore allows passive forms of investment but then also invites speculation (or "active" investment) based on the index itself, rather than merely its constituent elements.

This seems, therefore, to represent a technical refinement, or further stage, in the seemingly never ending arms race where liquid markets for securities, in whatever form, can create the potential for speculation, as a result of which short-term market values, and the hope of price appreciation, come to displace expectations of long-term yield.

Another drawback of passive investment, if based on an index like the stock market as a whole, is that there is no connection between the two worlds of financial investment and physical investment. Savings allocated to financial investment based on the stock market as a whole cannot be used for actual investment in new capital assets by the companies which make up that stock market. As we saw above, actual new capital brought to US companies through the stock market is a trivial proportion of the volume of stock trading which takes place – less than 1% annually. While passive investment might present advantages from the point of view of savers, and might perhaps present *indirect* advantages to quoted companies (if it results in less volatility in their traded shares), it does not in itself bridge the gap between savings and investment, or add to the very small proportion of new capital made available for these companies. For this to happen, a further stage is required, which we shall explore in Chapter Eight.

A role for the state?

To complete this chapter on savings and investment we should remind ourselves of the conclusion which Keynes himself arrived at in the *General Theory*. This was that, having taken into account the malfunctioning of private investment markets, the volatile state of long-term expectation, the tendency for "speculation" to overwhelm "enterprise" and the negative impact of all this on the current rate of investment (the crucial variable in the Keynesian analysis of the economy), the end result was not a good one. His view was: "*I conclude that the duty of ordering the current volume of investment cannot safely be left in private hands.*"

Keynes foresaw a role for the state which, by taking into account the long view and the general social advantage, should be able to do a better job of allocating investment in the economy than the fluctuating views of liquid investment markets. In later writings he suggested that the state could act as a coordinator of the various investment plans across the economy, for example by setting up a board of public investment, to cover areas like building, transport and public utilities, already lying half way between public and private control, to ensure sufficient investment comes on stream at any one time to maintain effective demand in the economy.[13]

Apart from after major financial crises (when it is still widely considered today to be the role of government to step in as an investor of last resort with extra public expenditure, on items like infrastructure) this idea of the state as a general regulator or controller of aggregate investment has rather been lost sight of. It perhaps deserves further examination, in the light of the discussion so far of knowledge, uncertainty and expectations.

If we accept Hayek's idea of the price system as being like a telecommunications system for transmitting useful practical knowledge around society in the short term, there seems little practical role for the state other than to ensure that the signals are not distorted, whether by the action of the state itself or by the action of private firms with some control over the market, either unilaterally or by means of cartels.

But with regard to long-term expectations, relating to a more distant and uncertain future, the position is rather different. It is not that the state has the ability to predict this more distant future better than any private firm. It is rather that private firms, collectively and interdependently, fluctuate in their expectations of the future (and hence the volume of investment they undertake) in ways which are too cyclical and erratic. In the absence of a workable theory of finance to allow reasonable estimates of the future, as might be found in other areas of science, the views of private parties tend to be subjective, to extrapolate too much from current circumstances and to reflect current, changeable, market sentiment. This may then suggest a role for the state (or a public body), not as a guide to the future, but rather to counterbalance the fluctuating views of the private sector – for example, by bringing public investment plans on stream where private plans fall short, and also reining back public plans where private plans are in full flow (since, as Keynes put it in the circumstances of 1937, *"the boom, not the slump, is the right time for procrastination at the Ministry of Health"*).[14]

In the view of Minsky, the US state should therefore be of a similar size to the volume of private investment in the US economy – precisely to offset the fluctuations caused by an unstable financial system.[15]

This is, of course, a difficult role to fulfil in practice, and becomes even more difficult when the issues are transposed from the national sphere to the international sphere, or to the world itself, given the global nature of today's financial markets and the interconnections of the global economy.

Nonetheless, unless and until a way can be found to stabilise private sector expectations, and therefore ensure a regular and smooth flow of savings into investment, some such method may yet need further examination. We will return to this point in later chapters.

Further recapitulation

The argument of this chapter might be summarised as follows. Uncertainty of the long-term future, which governs investment in new capital assets, and the use of savings in investment, is at present addressed by a method which can best and most charitably be described as pseudo-scientific. What is missing is a workable and falsifiable theory, such as might be found in other social or natural sciences which also deal with an uncertain future. The elements of such a theory could be based on the concept of forecasting yield from capital assets, which is a measurable phenomenon tending towards aggregate and long-term stability, and where there is a plentiful supply of historic data. A theory of this nature, allowing reasonable estimates and forecasts to be made, could be improved by a process of trial and error as time goes by. It also offers the prospect of a better matching of large-scale collective savings with investment, and less financial instability.

In the next chapter we will go on to look in more detail into how scientific theories and models fit together, both in general and in the specific case of economics.

Notes

1. Haldane A, "The Age of Asset Management?", speech 2014, Bank of England.
2. Minsky H, "Uncertainty and the Institutional Structure of Capitalist Economies", 1996, Working Paper No. 155, Jerome Levy Economics Institute of Bard College.
3. Bogle J, *The Clash of the Cultures*, 2012, Hoboken, New Jersey, John Wiley and Sons, page 5.
4. *The Clash of the Cultures*, page 44.
5. Soros G, *The Alchemy of Finance*, 1987, 1994, New York, John Wiley and Sons, page 29.
6. Reinhart C and Rogoff K, *This Time Is Different*, 2009, Princeton, New Jersey, Princeton University Press, page 150.
7. Keynes JM, *The General Theory of Employment, Interest and Money*, 1936, London, Macmillan, page 161.
8. Woolley P, *The Future of Finance*, 2010, London, School of Economics, page 134.
9. Popper K, *All Life is Problem Solving*, 1999, 2003, London, Routledge, page 3.
10. Blanchard O, Amighini A and Giavazzi F, *Macroeconomics: A European Perspective*, 2010, Harlow, Financial Times Prentice Hall, page 41.
11. Kay J, *Other People's Money*, 2015, London, Profile Books, page 161.
12. Bogle J, *The Clash of the Cultures*, 2012, Hoboken, New Jersey, John Wiley and Sons, page 168.
13. Keynes JM, "How to Avoid a Slump", 1937, Skidelsky R (Ed.), *The Essential Keynes*, 2015, London, Penguin, page 404.
14. *The Essential Keynes*, page 402.
15. Minsky H, *Stabilising an Unstable Economy*, 1986, 2008, New York, McGraw-Hill, page 330.

5   Models, theories and apples

How could a workable and falsifiable theory of finance fit into modern economics? In the mainstream economics of recent decades models of all kinds appear to have taken over the world. Examples include the DSGE ("dynamic stochastic general equilibrium") model used in economic forecasting, including by central banks, and the IS-LM ("investment, savings – liquidity, money") macroeconomic model (derived from, but not actually in, Keynes' *General Theory*). And supporting theories, including that expectations are rational and that markets are efficient, have underpinned the spectacular growth of finance.

As we saw in the previous chapter, Soros has proposed as an alternative to these his theory of reflexivity, which certainly seems to do a better job of explaining boom and bust patterns in financial markets, but at the expense of making a division between the social sciences and the natural sciences. If Soros is correct, the mistaken expectations which buoy up financial prices until they crash back to earth resemble distortions of reality promoted by unscrupulous politicians to advance their interests and gain positions of power. Postmodern manipulations of expectations – whether of prices in finance or of political reality – part company from the methods of natural science, and subjectivity triumphs over all. "Narratives" become more important than objective fundamentals (to borrow Mervyn King's expression).

Can we make sense of all this, and somehow put these jumbled concepts into order?

Popper, as a philosopher of science, maintained that there is actually no fundamental difference at all between the natural and social sciences. Both proceed by way of using theories in an attempt to solve problems, and subject theories to critical discussion and testing (or "falsification"). This is the "unity of method", the doctrine Popper put forward in *The Poverty of Historicism* in 1957.[1] (It is this doctrine which Soros does not accept.)

Popper pointed out that a characteristic of the social sciences is that most of its objects are abstract, or theoretical, constructions, which are embodied in the form of models, like models of institutions. (We talk readily in terms of "nations", or "constitutions", or "economies", but these are all abstract constructions. The institution of Parliament is not the physical building where Parliament resides. The institution of the rule of law is not the physical court of law.) But models are not unique to the social sciences, and are frequently used in the natural sciences as well (like models of atoms, molecules, solids and liquids), as part of the method of explaining by way of reduction, or deduction from hypotheses. As Popper remarked, "Very often we are unaware of the fact that we are operating with hypotheses or theories, and we therefore mistake our theoretical models for concrete things. This is a kind of mistake which is only too common."[2]

In the social science of economics, models are everywhere, but Popper thought models of this nature are really applications of theories to specific circumstances. The models of the theoretical social sciences are essentially descriptions or reconstructions of *typical* social situations. In fact, in his view, the idea of the social situation is fundamental to the methodology of the social sciences: "I should even be inclined to say that almost every problem of explanation in the social sciences requires an analysis of a social situation."[3]

Models and theories feature in both the natural and social sciences. As Popper put it, in relation to the former:

> Models, as here understood, may be called theories, or be said to incorporate theories, since they are attempts to solve problems – problems of explanation. But the opposite is far from true. Not all theories are models. Models represent typical initial conditions rather than universal laws. And they therefore need to be supplemented by 'animating' universal laws of interactions – by theories which are not models in the sense here indicated.[4]

So models are particular applications of theories to specific circumstances. We can illustrate this from everyday experience today. Models are used not just in economics but also outside economics (such as the highly complex computer models in today's climate science). And nor do all economic theories rely on models. The *General Theory* itself does not.

Rationality

Perhaps counter-intuitively, Popper also thought there are good reasons for believing that social sciences are less complicated than physics, and that concrete social situations are generally less complicated than concrete physical situations. This is because in most social situations there is an element of *rationality*. This is not to say that human beings always act with complete rationality (which they hardly ever do, in the sense of making the optimal use of all available information for the attainment of their ends), but they act, none the less, "more or less" rationally. It is this which makes it possible to construct "comparatively simple models of their actions and inter-actions, and to use these models as approximations."[5]

It is therefore this "more or less" rational behaviour which allows social sciences to construct the models which allow the testing of theories against reality to take place. One method is to construct a model on the assumption of complete rationality (and perhaps also on the assumption of the possession of complete information) on the part of all the individuals concerned, and then to estimate the deviation of actual behaviour of people from the model behaviour, using the latter as a kind of zero co-ordinate. In this way, Popper reasoned, in the field of economics comparisons could be made between actual behaviour and model behaviour to be expected on the basis of Hayek's idea of economics as the "logic of choice".[6] Or in industrial organisation theory, a comparison can be made between the "logic of large-scale operations" in industry and the "illogic of actual operations".

For Popper, then, rationality is a very useful principle of methodology in the social sciences, but not more than that. One might assume complete rationality, and the possession of complete information, when constructing models of various types, including in economics, but that is not the same as saying people really are completely rational or really possess complete information. It is the deviation of reality from the model which is interesting.

In "Models, Instruments and Truth" (based on a lecture in 1963 to the Harvard Department of Economics) Popper took pains to explain that the rationality principle in social sciences is both methodologically essential but also "false". What he meant was that, while it is false to say that everyone behaves rationally all the time, it is better to blame any breakdowns in models and theories in the social sciences on the models and theories themselves, rather than on the rationality principle. In that way, better models and theories can be arrived at.

Another way of expressing the point is to say it is too easy, and of little help, to fall back on irrationality as the explanation for anything. Moments of irrationality and collective madness no doubt exist, but if we want to create problem-solving models or theories in the social sciences we should presume that as a matter of course people behave "more or less" rationally.

"Rational expectations"

According to "rational expectations" theory, which has dominated modern mainstream macroeconomics for several decades, it is also to be assumed that the expectations held by people about the future course of the economy are held rationally, and that for any given economic policy, operators in the economy (those in financial markets, those in the real economy and consumers themselves) will use the information they have in the best possible way. On the face of it, this is similar to the "zero co-ordinate" method of constructing models as described by Popper, above. In itself, as a way of building an economic model, it is perfectly unobjectionable.

The difficulty arises if the model comes to displace reality – the "*kind of mistake which is only too common*", as Popper remarked. The risk of doing this can be seen in the origins of rational expectations theory, usually ascribed to the US economist John Muth, writing in 1961 ("Rational Expectations and the Theory of Price Movements"[7]). According to Muth:

> I should like to suggest that expectations, since they are informed predictions of future events, are essentially the same as the predictions of the relevant economic theory [...] [This can be rephrased to say] that expectations of

businesses [...] tend to be distributed, for the same information set, about the prediction of the theory [...].

The impact of this approach has been tremendous. To quote from a recent (2010) textbook on macroeconomics:

> Most macroeconomists today routinely solve their models under the assumption of rational expectations. This was not always the case. The past 35 years in macroeconomic research are often called the 'rational expectations revolution'.[8]

What does this mean, exactly? If the assumption of rational expectations were simply that, for the purposes of constructing any given model, individuals behave with complete rationality, and are in possession of complete information, that would be consistent with Popper's suggestion that such a model can be a "zero co-ordinate", against which real behaviour in the economy can be measured.

But rational expectations theory goes further than this. It suggests that both on the aggregate, or macro, level and on the individual, or micro, level the expectations held by operators in the economy are "essentially the same" as the predictions of economic theory. In this way expectations and economic theory become fused, and hard to disentangle from each other.

To see how this works out in practice, consider the following example from the same macroeconomic textbook, explaining how rational expectations might work in a scenario involving an announcement by the government that there is to be a reduction in its deficit:

> The way this is likely to happen: forecasts by economists will show that these lower deficits are likely to lead to higher output and lower interest rates in the future. In response to these forecasts, long-term interest rates will decrease, and the stock market will increase. People and firms, reading these forecasts and looking at bond and stock prices, will revise their spending plans and increase spending.[9]

The "rationality" of rational expectations theory becomes, then, the degree to which expectations conform to what economic theory predicts. And how do people and firms discover what these predictions are? Like this:

> We can think of [managers of mutual funds, firms deciding whether to invest and consumers deciding whether to save] as forming expectations about the future by assessing the likely course of future expected policy and then working out the implications for future activity. If they do not do it themselves (surely most of us do not spend our time solving macroeconomic models before making decisions), they do so indirectly by watching TV and reading newsletters and newspapers, which in turn rely on the forecasts of public and private forecasters. Economists refer to expectations formed in this forward-looking manner as rational expectations.[10]

"Rational expectations" do not just affect large-scale aggregate macroeconomic thinking, where the question is what the impact of changes in government economic policy will be. They also permeate thinking and policy about the behaviour of individual firms in the economy, in particular firms operating in financial markets. Thus, in foreign exchange markets, it has been said that the rational expectations approach "implies that if a particular model is used to explain market behaviour, it should also be assumed that the market formed its expectations on the basis of the same model."[11]

Financial regulation itself was for years rooted in the theory of efficient and "rational" markets. When reviewing the fundamental theoretical issues underpinning financial regulation in the UK before the 2008 financial crisis, the 2009 Turner Review of the UK Financial Services Authority observed that at the core of the intellectual assumptions on which financial regulation had hitherto been based was the theory of efficient and rational markets. And the first proposition of all was that "Market prices are good indicators of rationally evaluated economic value."[12]

Great expectations

When we step back and consider all this from the point of view of Popper's theory of knowledge we can see the difficulties.

First, models and theories risk becoming mistaken for reality – an "only too common" mistake in science. Some economic operators might have expectations which are the same as whatever the "relevant economic theory" predicts, but others evidently do not. As we saw in Chapter Three, surveys indicate that the actual expectations of those responsible for making the investment decisions of large US companies are based largely on an extrapolation of their own company earnings in the previous twelve months. It cannot be assumed that reality will conform to the predictions of economic theory. This could only happen under certain very tightly controlled laboratory circumstances – Popper's "zero co-ordinate".

Second, and at a deeper level, "rational expectations" do not permit expectations of the future to be tested by a trial and error method. If we recall the position in earlier chapters, it is of the essence in Popper's view of both the natural and social sciences that the future is open, and not determined by the past. Expectations, usually based on previously observed regularities, certainly exist, but they are no more than hypotheses, or guesses. Knowledge grows by the testing of expectations against reality, and the creation of theories to explain the discrepancies. In economic terms, and in the language of Knight and Keynes, openness can be expressed as uncertainty, an uncertainty which increases the further ahead in time we look. But "rational expectations" exclude an open, or uncertain, future, which means that knowledge itself cannot grow. Expectations may be perfectly "rational", or reasonable, and yet also prove to be perfectly wrong. The assumption that the future will be a simple extension of the present creates an excessive rigidity, which perhaps explains why so many complex economic models do not appear to work.[13]

Third, even if heroic assumptions of rational expectations might have a use for modelling purposes, where the question is understanding the impact of economic policy on the aggregate behaviour of large groups of the population, this does not help us when we turn to the individual pricing decisions taken by firms in the economy. Here, so far as finance is concerned, it is no doubt the conjunction of the twin ideas that financial markets are both "efficient" and "rational" which is the root of the problem. ("Efficient" here means that prices in financial markets incorporate all relevant information.) Markets which are both "efficient" and "rational" will naturally require little, if any, supervision, and financial regulation can afford to be light-touch, or minimal. Repeated financial crashes and instability will, by definition, not arise.

The two-price system explanation of the economy adopted in this book indicates why this is not the case.

In the first price system, in the real economy, prices normally result from a relatively short-term process where producers of current output aim to cover costs, plus a margin for profit, when they sell products, in the shape of goods and services, on to purchasers. Producers may well have reasonable and well-founded expectations of what price they might be able to achieve, but they cannot know for certain until the sale process is concluded. It does not really matter whether their expectations are rational or totally irrational (wildly over-optimistic, for example): it is the trial and error process of the price mechanism in a competitive market economy which determines if they are correct.

By contrast, a different logic is in play in financial markets. Here, prices are valuing income flows (yields) from outstanding capital and financial assets. These income flows are of a long-term nature, but prices at any one moment fluctuate in the light of a myriad of factors affecting the relative views of those buying and selling in financial markets. If a sufficient number of market participants took a long-term view, and were interested in the long-term income flows from capital and financial assets, financial prices might perhaps tend towards stability. However, experience suggests that, as financial markets become bigger and more liquid, Keynesian "speculation" (attempting to forecast the short-term psychology of the market) has more impact than "enterprise" (attempting to make reasonable estimates of the long-term yield of capital assets), leading to erratic and volatile financial prices, and at the extreme to booms and crashes. This explanation of how financial prices are formed does not suggest they will be good indicators of "rationally evaluated" economic value. Rather the contrary – they will simply be good indicators of the shifting collective view of market participants of an uncertain future. Equilibrium, like Godot, will never arrive.

A realistic approach to expectations in economics would therefore treat them much as expectations in any other social or natural science. They may be "informed predictions", and happily correct – or they may, on the other hand, be completely wrong.

Back to the unity of method

What would it mean for financial economics to revert to being a social or natural science like any other? For a start, we should recall Popper's emphasis on science being a problem-solving activity. Without understanding the problem situation that gives rise to a theory, a theory is pointless – it cannot be properly understood. For example, "without understanding the problems raised by depression and unemployment for neo-classical economics, Keynes' theory must appear pointless, and cannot be fully understood."[14]

It would also mean that, as in other sciences, uncertainty must be taken seriously. There comes a point where the near-term future stretches into the long-term future and, as to what might happen, as Keynes said, "*We simply do not know.*" This should not be revolutionary: it is the basis on which the rest of science operates. It is possible to create scientific theories which predict what might happen in the future, sometimes with an astonishing degree of accuracy (the motions of the planets, for example); but these theories, even the best and most sophisticated, are always tentative and provisional, never providing complete certainty. Popper was emphatic that there is no determinism, even in the most advanced physical sciences.

If it is unsettling for financial economics to come to terms with genuine uncertainty, there may be comfort to be taken from Popper's remark that the social sciences should actually be less complicated than the physical sciences, because in them there is usually an element of rationality. This is not the same as saying there is perfect rationality (or the rationality of "rational expectations"), but rather there is enough of the "more or less" rationality to allow comparatively simple models to be created, and tested. (We should recall that Popper was greatly impressed by the incredible complexity of the physical universe, and how the growth of scientific knowledge reveals the depth of our ignorance.)

In the market economy – including the two price systems we have encountered – an assumption that people behave "more or less" rationally seems in fact correct. But they do so in the social situation they find themselves (for example, the institutions and rules of the market they happen to be in). Popper suggested that at the root of most problems of explanation in the social sciences is an understanding of the social situation. And in finance it is almost impossible to understand the dynamics of capital markets without understanding the role of institutional investors, their relationship to collective savings, the way in which all the various parties are remunerated, and the incentives they face. Behaviour nearly always turns out to be "more or less" rational in the prevailing circumstances. (Moments of complete panic, and collective madness, can certainly be found, such as in financial crashes, but, as in most crises, the problem is usually one of finding out what is going on at a time of extreme uncertainty, and an inability to distinguish true from false information. This is not irrational.)

Moreover, if it is the case that "more or less" rationality prevails, even in financial economics, that indicates the possibility of reform and improvement, which does not presuppose perfect rationality but which – as in other areas of social science – addresses practical problems as they arise. The supposed dichotomy in economics between "rational" and "irrational" behaviour becomes unnecessary, and in fact alien to the ethos of the open society, and the normal scientific method.

To illustrate the issues, let us reflect on the position of three different apples.

Three views of an apple

Newton's apple can be taken to illustrate the physical sciences. The well-known story, possibly apocryphal, goes as follows:

> Whilst [Sir Isaac Newton] was pensively meandering in a garden it came into his thought that the power of gravity (which brought an apple from a tree to the ground) was not limited to a certain distance from earth, but that this power must extend much further than was usually thought. Why not as high as the Moon said he to himself & if so, that must influence her motion & perhaps retain her in her orbit, whereupon he fell a calculating what would be the effect of that supposition.[15]

What does this famous anecdote tell us? That Newton envisaged a force of attraction (the power of gravity) which operates at a distance, and extends not just from the ground to an apple up in a tree, but from the earth to the moon. The power of gravity extends across empty space, and is also transmitted not just from the earth to the moon, but from the sun to the earth, and to all the other planets. The force of attraction is greater with the mass of the object, and diminishes with distance (in fact it is the inverse square of the distance between two objects). Newtonian calculations of the competing influences of gravity on the objects of the solar system provide an explanation of where those objects are, and a prediction where they will be in future, in use to this day.

The Newtonian theory of gravity as a universal force of attraction is more or less the toast of the physical sciences. Within it, the apple sits as a tiny object subject to calculable influences, representing on a small scale the dynamics which apply in the solar system, and in the entire galaxy beyond.

Nonetheless, for all its influence, it is worth noting the theory is wrong, or at least incomplete. According to Einstein's general theory of relativity, gravity is actually the curved geometry of space-time. This does not affect our little apple in any appreciable way: but it does show how even the best scientific theories are tentative approximations, not providing certainty.

Next, we should look at Popper's apple. In "A World of Propensities: Two New Views of Causality", based on a lecture given to the World Congress of Philosophy in 1988, Popper developed the idea of propensities as a refinement of probability theory, which explain how new and more complex states can emerge from existing orders. Popper observed as follows:

> Real apples are emphatically not Newtonian apples. They fall usually when the wind blows. And the whole process is initiated by a biochemical process that weakens the stem so that the often-repeated movement due to the wind, together with the Newtonian weight of the apple, leads to a snap of the stem – a process we can analyse but cannot calculate in detail, mainly because of the probabilistic character of the biochemical processes that prevents us from predicting what will happen in a unique situation. What we might be able to calculate is the propensity of a special type of apple to fall within, say, the

next hour. That may make it possible for us to predict that, if the weather deteriorates, it will very probably fall within the next week. There is no determinism in Newton's falling apple if we look at it realistically. And much less in many of our changing states of mind, for example in our so-called motives.[16]

What is Popper getting at here? He is illustrating the point that scientific experiments, held under laboratory conditions, usually have to exclude disturbing extraneous influences if they are to produce results which can be repeated at will. While the system of planets in our solar system is well isolated from all external mechanical influence, and therefore is a unique, natural, laboratory experiment, here on earth – where the real apples are – we have much greater difficulty in isolating the subject for study. In words recalling his "zero co-ordinate" approach in the social sciences, above, he remarked:

> Now, how are such theories [in the physical sciences] tested? Obviously by making experiments. And this means: by creating, at will, artificial conditions that either exclude, or reduce to zero, all the interfering and disturbing propensities.

Popper's "world of propensities" is a world where possibilities realise themselves creatively, provided they have enough time. Propensities are weighted possibilities, which repeat themselves statistically, and tend towards stability. Popper's apple has a "propensity" to fall, but we cannot be sure exactly when.

Finally, let us take Keynes' apple. Keynes admired Newton and acquired an important collection of Newton papers, including the very account of the apple incident set out above. When arguing against an over-mechanical use of statistics, Keynes wrote as follows in a letter of 1938 to the economist Roy Harrod:

> I also want to emphasise strongly the point about economics being a moral science. I mentioned before that it deals with introspection and with values. I might have added that it deals with motives, expectations, psychological uncertainties. One has to be constantly on guard against treating the material as constant and homogenous. It is as though the fall of the apple to the ground depended on the apple's motives, on whether it is worth while falling to the ground, and whether the ground wanted the apple to fall, and on mistaken calculations on the part of the apple as to how far it was from the centre of the earth.[17]

Keynes' apple is animated – it has hopes and expectations. And so does the ground on which it falls. Mistakes can be made. There is nothing mechanistic, or deterministic, in the economic forces at work. And because the material of economics is not constant and homogenous it is dangerous to rely on models which assume it is.

So an apple can be the subject of interplanetary forces; be part of a biochemical process; or be the Hamlet-like mistaken and introspective author of its own downfall. The natural and social (and moral) sciences are all part of a continuum, blending into each other. Nor should we forget that the apple tree itself may also have a part to play in the great drama: Popper was open to the idea that trees might have knowledge too, as well as animals. Trees have a long life, and might well have their own long-term expectations of the seasonal changes that affect them, and cause them to shed their apples. As the title of one of Popper's books has it, *"All Life is Problem Solving"*.

Back to the future

What does it mean to take uncertainty seriously? Let us revisit Keynes' famous remark from 1937:

> The sense in which I am using the term [of uncertain knowledge] is that in which the prospect of a European war is uncertain, or the price of copper and the rate of interest twenty years hence, or the obsolescence of a new invention, or the position of private wealth-owners in the social system in 1970. About these matters there is no scientific basis on which to form any calculable probability whatever. We simply do not know.[18]

Keynes was talking about the application of uncertain knowledge of the future to the economic activity of the accumulation of wealth. He went on to say that while classical economic theory might work very well in a world in which economic goods are consumed within a short interval of their being produced (the first price system in a two-price market economy, as described above), it needs considerable amendment to a world where the accumulation of wealth for an indefinitely postponed future is an important factor. And the greater the role of such accumulation the more amendment to classical economic theory is necessary.

We should pause on Keynes' words "no scientific basis on which to form any calculable probability whatever". This is like Popper's remark, in respect of an apple, that the physical sciences can analyse the biochemical process that will lead to it falling from a stem, but are in no position to predict what will happen in future in a unique situation. While Keynes' subject of the accumulation of wealth presents difficulties if we try to make accurate predictions of specific future events, broad trends and "propensities" can nonetheless be discerned. Reasonable forecasts of certain matters, based on experience and previously observed regularities, can also be made. Examples would include the effect of compound interest, the rate of growth of savings, and the yield of capital assets. The average real rate of return on capital appears to be a broadly constant figure over the long term. Probabilities may not be calculable but propensities may. We know that apples in general will fall in autumn. A workable and falsifiable theory of yields of capital assets might, indeed, amend classical economic theory; but only by bringing it into the realm of the rest of science.

(It is, incidentally, the distinction between relatively stable long-term economic trends and the short-term erratic behaviour of financial markets which forms the heart of Alan Greenspan's interesting post-crash revisionist account of the difficulties of economic forecasting, *The Map and the Territory* (2013).)[19]

What, then, of Keynes' point that economics deals with "motives, expectations, psychological uncertainties"? Like Popper, he is saying that as a moral science it is not deterministic. (Popper would say the physical sciences are not deterministic either.) Economic models and statistical methods which assume constancy and homogeneity in their extrapolations can be dangerously misleading. Since the future is open, and undetermined, they need watching assiduously. They may be good servants, but make bad masters once they exclude possible futures.

Popper's point that in the social sciences behaviour is likely to be "more or less" rational should, however, limit even economics from going completely off the rails. Mistakes can be made but knowledge can grow. Keynes' "madmen in authority, who hear voices in the air", may to this day distil their frenzy from some academic scribbler of a few years back. But, in an open society, the gradual encroachment of ideas should, eventually, discipline unreason.

It is with this in mind that in the next few chapters we will look at some possible public policy answers to the problems of finance raised so far in this book.

Notes

1. Popper K, *The Poverty of Historicism*, 1957, 1991, London, Routledge, page 139.
2. *The Poverty of Historicism*, page 136.
3. Popper K, *The Myth of the Framework*, 1994, 1996, London, Routledge, page 166.
4. *The Myth of the Framework*, page 165.
5. *The Poverty of Historicism*, page 140.
6. *The Poverty of Historicism*, page 141.
7. Muth J, "Rational Expectations and the Theory of Price Movements", 1961, *Econometrica*, 29, 3: pages 315–335.
8. Blanchard O, Amighini A and Giavazzi F, *Macroeconomics: A European Perspective*, 2010, Harlow, Financial Times Prentice Hall, page 355.
9. *Macroeconomics: A European Perspective*, page 357.
10. *Macroeconomics: A European Perspective*, page 355.
11. Grabbe J, *International Financial Markets*, 1986, New York, Elsevier, page 157.
12. Turner A, *The Turner Review: A Regulatory Response to the Global Banking Crisis*, 2009, London, Financial Services Authority.
13. Buiter W, "The Unfortunate Uselessness of Most 'State of the Art' Academic Monetary Economics", 2009, *Munich Personal RePec Archives*.
14. *The Myth of the Framework*, page 157.
15. As recounted by John Conduitt, Newton's assistant at the Royal Mint, in his draft account of Newton's life, in the Keynes Ms 130.4, King's College, Cambridge.
16. Popper K, *A World of Propensities*, 1990, Bristol, Thoemmes Press, page 24.
17. Skidelsky R (Ed.), *The Essential Keynes*, 2015, London, Penguin, page 281.
18. Keynes JM, "The General Theory of Employment", 1937, Skidelsky R (Ed.), *The Essential Keynes*, London, Penguin, page 265.
19. Greenspan A, *The Map and the Territory*, 2013, London, Allen Lane.

6 Policy implications – finance

If we move from the realm of theory to the practicalities of the real world what then can we see?

Openness, and indeed an open society, implies the future is always and necessarily uncertain. This is inevitable. But, in the words of Hyman Minsky: "*The impact of Money Manager Capitalism is heightening uncertainty.*" Minsky thought that institutional innovations which help offset the impact of uncertainty would be needed, as the losers in the gamble imposed by uncertainty can become alienated and potential recruits for an alternative to democracy.[1]

Minsky was referring to the tendency of "money manager capitalism" (today's system where most financial instruments are held by institutional investors) to demand constant short-term profits, regardless of the long-term effects on businesses and employees. The "gamble imposed by uncertainty" is the betting which takes place when funds are shifted from one investment to the next in the hope of a better immediate short-term return.

Since the loss of a global monetary standard in 1971, global growth has diminished and uncertainty increased (dramatically so when international prices, like that of oil, suddenly lose their moorings). But the market mechanisms used for dealing with uncertainty – borrowed from trading arrangements found in the real exchange economy – appear to be inadequate. This is because, too often, as financial markets develop and become bigger and more liquid, the forces of "speculation" within them (attempting to forecast the psychology of the market) overtake the forces of "enterprise" (attempting to make reasonable estimates of the long-term yield of capital assets). The consequence is that uncertainty is not corrected by these markets, but magnified.

Thus, international currencies have fluctuated more than anticipated when Bretton Woods was ended, driven by fluctuating short-term expectations in the huge inter-bank foreign exchange market, rather than by adjustments to economic fundamentals. (The original theory, that floating exchange rates would stabilise and come into balance, as the price of traded goods between countries moved towards purchasing power parity, has not come to pass.)

Stock prices have been volatile, driven by short-term speculation over the value of assets in liquid markets rather than any serious attempt to estimate underlying yields, or channel savings into investment. (There is, moreover, a link with rising inequality: remuneration tied to stock prices – as with senior management in the US – will diverge from normal employee pay when stock prices diverge from the underlying earnings of companies. This underlies the analysis of rising inequality in the US to be found in Piketty's *Capital in the Twenty-First Century*.)

The prices of capital assets in the shape of property have also been distorted by excessive bank credit when over-optimistic expectations are transmitted between lenders. The Japanese property bubble and its crash in 1990, and the global property bubble and crash in 2008, are the most spectacular recent examples.

If uncertainty cannot be avoided completely can it be made manageable? Reduced to the minimum? Until the 1970s, the Bretton Woods system provided a relatively stable framework giving a measure of predictability for the expanding post-war world economy. International currencies were linked to the dollar, and the dollar was linked to gold. Former Federal Reserve chairman Paul Volcker called this "a more orderly, rule-based world of financial stability, and close cooperation among nations".[2] Jacques de Larosière (former managing director of the IMF) has explained how the discipline of a fixed exchange rate regime curtailed the excessive creation of credit around the world (and therefore of debt).[3] What, then, is the alternative now?

A dance to the music of time

In the various examples above, prices shift not because underlying fundamentals shift but because expectations in the market shift, insufficiently grounded in objective reality (like yields of capital assets, or, in the case of currencies, the economic situation of entire countries). Keynes called this phenomenon a "conventional basis of valuation" – a valuation not rooted in fundamentals, but in the current conventional opinion of the market. He also warned of its dangers:

> In particular, being based on so flimsy a foundation, it is subject to sudden and violent changes. The practice of calmness and immobility, of certainty and security, suddenly breaks down. New fears and hopes will, without warning, take charge of human conduct. The forces of disillusion may suddenly impose a new conventional basis of valuation.[4]

These price shifts include the modern concept of "momentum" trading, involving swings amplifying price movements. Once sufficient funds become drawn in behind a price swing it appears practically impossible for participants taking an opposing view to correct it. In foreign exchange, as Roosa put it, "the sea of fluid currencies [...] is so large that the resulting exchange rate changes can appear as tidal waves".[5] In stocks, Woolley cites the example of the dotcom bubble in the 1999–2000 period, when funds were withdrawn from investment managers sceptical of the technology bubble in favour of those going with the trend, as a result pushing stock prices higher – until they collapsed. And in the case of bank credit before the 2008 financial crisis, the words of the then Chief Executive of

Citigroup are legendary: "When the music stops, in terms of liquidity, things will be complicated. But as long as the music is playing, you've got to get up and dance. We're still dancing."[6]

The impossibility for individual participants to resist the music and momentum of the market means that corrections do not take place gradually and smoothly, but abruptly and only after prices have been dragged in one direction or another. As Keynes described it in the *General Theory*, with memories of the financial crisis of 1929 still fresh:

> It is of the nature of organised investment markets, under the influence of purchasers largely ignorant of what they are buying and of speculators who are more concerned with forecasting the next shift of market sentiment than with a reasonable estimate of the future yield of capital-assets, that, when disillusion falls upon an over-optimistic and over-bought market, it should fall with sudden and even catastrophic force.[7]

The *General Theory* bristles with warnings like this. From the above passage (taken from Chapter Twenty-Two ("Notes on the Trade Cycle")), to the famous remark in Chapter Twelve ("The State of Long-Term Expectation") that "the position is serious when enterprise becomes a bubble on a whirlpool of speculation. When the capital development of a country becomes a by-product of the activities of a casino, the job is likely to be ill-done", the theme of instability in organised financial markets recurs time and again.

So why have Keynes' insights from the *General Theory* been lost, or ignored? The beginning of the Second World War, shortly after publication in 1936, may have made concerns about the operation of the peace time economy redundant; and then the war-time agreement in 1944 on the Bretton Woods system (in which Keynes, of course, played a prominent role) created the post-war conditions for relative international monetary and financial stability. Within the US, as Minsky has pointed out, banking and finance in the immediate post-war decades were largely taken up with handling the large overhang of government debt from the war. It was not until the 1960s that banks began to speculate actively with respect to their liabilities.[8] The convenient new doctrines that financial markets are both efficient and rational provided the backdrop to the liberalisation of finance that followed.

We are, therefore, now, after the crisis of 2008, somewhere near the position Keynes was in the 1930s when surveying the period after the 1929 crash and the ensuing Depression. Convenient doctrines and beliefs have failed.

To help us here, a further point about Keynes and "Keynesianism" may be worth making. "Keynesianism" today is usually taken to mean deficit-financing, or the state carrying out public works (typically the construction of infrastructure) to offset a downturn in private investment, particularly after a financial crisis. While this remedy can be found in the *General Theory*, more fundamental is the diagnosis behind the crises in the first place. It is with "markets organised and influenced as they are at present" that the "enormously wide fluctuations" in the market estimation of the marginal efficiency of capital can arise, too great to be offset by changes in the interest rate:

> In conditions of laissez-faire the avoidance of wide fluctuations in employment may, therefore, prove impossible without a far-reaching change in the psychology of investment markets such as there is no reason to expect. I conclude that the duty of ordering the current volume of investment cannot safely be left in private hands.[9]

Keynes later wrote that, while the diagnosis explaining why output and employment are so liable to fluctuate set out in the *General Theory* was meant to be definitive, the suggestions for a cure "are not meant to be definitive; they are subject to all sorts of special assumptions and are necessarily related to the particular conditions of the time".[10]

We are free, then, to devise cures for shortfalls in the current volume of investment as we wish, to suit the particular conditions of the prevailing circumstances. But it is the underlying untreated ailment which is the problem: the "psychology" of investment markets is still defective, and has not yet been subject to far-reaching change.

Breaking with convention

Several promising initiatives are, however, under way around the world in the wake of the 2008 financial crisis, in an attempt to curb short-termism in finance, as a manifestation of this psychological defect.

One is the "Focusing Capital on the Long Term" international movement, including businesses, institutional investors, pension funds and advisers, whose objective since inception in 2013 has been to encourage institutional investors to develop ways of taking into account the long-term value of companies, rather than relying on the share price. It is suggested that long-term asset managers could, for example, depending on the industry, pay more attention to companies' ten-year economic value added; R&D efficiency; patent pipeline; multiyear returns on capital investments; or energy intensity. These are all measurements of the long-term value of companies. In 2016 the Canada Pension Plan Investment Board, together with S & P Dow Jones Indices, launched a new S & P Long-Term Value Creation Global Index, designed to track those companies that seek to create long-term value, and provide a benchmark index for investors.

In the US, Bogle has put forward several proposals to curb what he has described as "the dominance of today's counterproductive speculative orientation" in the investment industry. Notable among these is the enactment of a federal standard of fiduciary duty for investment professionals, requiring a long-term investment focus; due diligence in security selection; participation in corporate affairs; reasonable costs; and the elimination of conflicts of interest.[11] In 2016 the US government proposed a new fiduciary standard applicable to advisers of US pension schemes.

In the UK, the work at the London School of Economics of the Paul Woolley Centre for Capital Market Dysfunctionality has focused on how the operation of the asset management industry produces results in global capital markets bearing little relation to the suppositions of the efficient market hypothesis. Pointing out that it is the flow of funds between asset managers which distorts asset prices through momentum effects, former fund manager Woolley and his colleagues suggest that the solution is for end users (the savers who are the principals) to take greater control over the fund managers (their agents) to ensure they take a long-term view, and that fund managers are rewarded by their investment performance over the long term, rather than by reference to faulty market price benchmarks.[12]

In "A Vision for Real Estate Finance in the UK" (2014), a cross-industry real estate finance group in London has explored practical methods for dampening commercial property price instability, by adopting long-term valuations when using commercial property as collateral for bank lending.[13]

The economist Andrew Smithers (on the Advisory Board of the Paul Woolley Centre) has drawn attention to the effects of low productivity and low levels of investment on industry generally, and linked these to bonus schemes for senior executives which dissuade long-term investment because they seek high short-term stock prices instead:

> As we need more investment and lower profit margins, we should aim to make it in the interests of management that the companies they manage spend heavily in new capital and keep prices down in order to win market share. If that seems impossible, we should at least try to reduce the current incentives that encourage less investment and higher margins.[14]

Through these, and other, ways, thought and analysis is being devoted to the mechanics of the savings/investment relationship, and how fluctuating and erratic prices in financial and capital asset markets can provide misleading signals to real economy markets, and the commercial and investment decisions taken by the companies that create new economic wealth. The chain of logic is compelling: if companies do not invest there will be low productivity, and if there is low productivity there will be poorly paid jobs and economic stagnation. If finance-driven time horizons become too short, long-term investment decreases.

If we step back and consider all this in the light of the impact of genuine uncertainty on economic behaviour can we see a way of supporting these initiatives?

Keynes' starting point, when explaining how the phenomenon of the "conventional basis of valuation" arises, is that it is really a normal reaction to uncertainty of the future:

> Knowing that our individual judgment is worthless, we endeavour to fall back on the judgment of the rest of the world which is perhaps better informed. That is, we endeavour to conform with the behaviour of the majority or the average. The psychology of a society of individuals each of whom is endeavouring to copy the others leads to what we may strictly term a conventional judgment.[15]

If we cannot expect short-term trading arrangements in financial markets to provide the answer to uncertainty – because, in essence, everyone in them is trying to copy everyone else – what then can we do?

What appears to be missing is an anchor for expectations, to reduce the level of uncertainty to the minimum. Such an anchor need not be permanently fixed, or unchangeable: but it does need to be more reliable and stable than the expectations of firms, otherwise driven in liquid markets by the short-term activity of forecasting one another, and the collective sentiment of the market. This is only likely to happen through an agreed public policy, transmitted via a common rule or standard: it is unlikely to arise spontaneously.

It is for this reason, in retrospect, that the Bretton Woods arrangements were valuable, and better than the arrangements that have succeeded them. It is not that a gold-based currency system was perfect, or that a better monetary standard could not be envisaged: it is rather that, in the absence of any internationally agreed and accepted standard, one will not create itself out of thin air, as values swing erratically between private parties, engaged in a competitive process.

Financial price stability

One logical answer therefore is to treat fluctuating financial and capital asset prices in a similar way to real economy prices, and extend to them the general public policy objective of an expectation of relative price stability.

What are the advantages in doing so? There is, for a start, no obvious public interest in asset price instability. On the contrary: as we saw in Chapter One, sudden shifts in asset prices have been the precursor to too many expensive financial crises around the world in recent decades, with devastating economic and political consequences. The problem is usually at its worst when credit is involved in the purchase (or refinancing) of assets like property, and a collapse in the price creates an overhang of unserviceable debt, or severely weakens the banking system. For this reason alone, relative price stability would be a public good.

A second advantage involves revisiting Keynes' concept of the marginal efficiency of capital, introduced in Chapter Three. It is the "enormously wide" fluctuations in the market estimation of the marginal efficiency of capital, in booms and busts, which generate the fluctuations in output and employment which form the macroeconomics of the *General Theory*. At the level of an individual firm, the marginal efficiency of capital consists of two factors: the supply price of a capital asset (a current, known, price) and also the prospective yield (stream of income) to be obtained from that capital asset, throughout its whole life, as if it were a series of annuities. This second factor is more uncertain, as it is based on expectations, which fluctuate in line with market expectations of the marginal efficiency of the capital. However, if expectations of the prospective yield of capital assets could be stabilised (because asset prices in general are expected to become more stable), that should make the investment decisions of firms in new capital assets easier to take, so increasing levels of investment and therefore of productivity. This would, in other words, be a counter to short-termism. To adopt the more recent analysis of Andrew Smithers, company executives would have reduced incentives to seek short-term high share prices (for example, through company share buy-backs), and more incentive to concentrate on longer-term investment.

A third advantage is for long-term savers, in particular in the pooled savings funds which have developed since Keynes' time and which dominate today's investment industry. A focus based on yields of savings funds, with less costly shifting of funds through momentum trading from one investment to the next, should result from greater asset price stability. Momentum effects should diminish, as there is less reason for intermediaries to exploit short-term price differences. Rewards for long-term performance should become easier to measure, and a better matching of the long-term liabilities of large savings funds, such as pension funds, with the long-term yields of their assets.

A fourth advantage would be to curb a significant cause of rising inequality, which is the divergence between remuneration linked to financial prices (like options on stock) and remuneration linked to the actual earnings of the same companies from sales (normal employee pay). In other words, financial prices have been rising more than real economy prices. Piketty's *Capital in the Twenty-First Century* draws attention to the distorting effects of the remuneration of a stratum of "supermanagers", as the main source of income inequality in the US since the 1970s: "the increase in the prosperity of high-earning Americans is explained primarily by the skyrocketing pay packages of top managers of large firms in the nonfinancial as well as financial sectors." Within these packages, the value of stock options "has played an important role in the increase of wage inequality".[16]

A final advantage of price stability should be to limit the random effects of Minsky's "gamble imposed by uncertainty" under money manager capitalism, with the losers becoming alienated and possible recruits for an alternative to democracy. The arbitrary consequences of the short-term profit-seeking of money managers, shifting funds from one investment to the next to maximise fund-holder value through higher stock prices, should be reduced in a more stable world where there are fewer price differentials, and investment is more for the longer term. Minsky describes how money manager capitalism has heightened uncertainty at US firm and plant level, in particular for middle management, with historic patterns of firm paternalism unravelling, and a chronic need to downsize overheads and to seek out least expensive variable cost. These pressures should be reduced in a regime of price stability, with uncertainty reduced.

Should price stability extend to all financial and asset prices everywhere; or would general or aggregate price stability suffice? Just as in the real economy, where hardly any individual prices are actually controlled on public policy grounds, it seems unnecessary and unrealistic to attempt to stabilise all individual financial prices. Aggregate and relative price stability, either across the board or within certain groups or baskets of assets, should be easier to attain. Price stability would not mean price rigidity; but rather that increases in prices should be in line with underlying long-term yields.

The source of financial price instability should also be recalled here: it arises where buyers and sellers do not balance out, but there is an excess of one class or the other, backed by a sufficient volume of funds, copying one another and moving prices up or down. This appears to be possible under virtually any circumstances in any liquid markets, irrespective of the underlying asset being valued, indicating that under conditions of uncertainty it is the copying behaviour itself (the "conventional basis of valuation") which is the problem. We will return to this subject in the next chapter.

Stabilising an unstable world

If financial and asset price stability can be a general public good, with significant advantages, how might it be achieved in practice? A number of different ways of approaching the problem can be conceived. We can focus here on three important areas, which are stock prices; capital assets in the shape of property; and international currencies. The market for each is different, but they share the common characteristic that, through speculation, prices can diverge from underlying fundamentals.

What are stock prices? As Keynes said, they are the values attributed to already existing capital assets (or titles to them, in the form of securities issued by companies). Changes in stock prices are revaluations of already existing capital assets, driven not by actual physical changes in those capital assets but by shifting expectations of financial intermediaries in the market. It is action in relation to those expectations which therefore matters (more so than in real economy markets, where producer prices are closely linked to the costs of production).

However, the long-term yields from capital assets prove to be comparatively stable. This is the case on average, over the long term, and also for large well-established companies, whose real economic value broadly tracks the health of the economy as a whole. As we saw in Chapter Four, returns for US companies over the previous 150 years are available, and show that dividend yields and real earnings growth aggregate at about 7% annually.

To anchor price expectations, then, one method would be to compile and publish data on the actual historic yields of the capital assets (or companies) in question, over as long a period of data as is available. Shifts in stock prices (valuing exactly the same existing capital assets) which are out of line with underlying historical trends can be taken to indicate price instability, and that expectations need adjusting to reality.

Who should be responsible for doing this? The obvious candidates are central banks, already as a general rule committed to a policy of price stability in the real economy. It is usually objected that, even if they wanted to, central banks cannot use their main instrument of setting interest rates to cope with asset price bubbles, since that would be counterproductive for the rest of the real economy. This is true, and Keynes pointed out (above) that in any event changes in interest rates may not offset wide fluctuations in market estimates of the marginal efficiency of capital. However, setting a framework of expectations, backed by evidence, is exactly what central banks can do. And, since stock prices are today globally interconnected and correlated, due to the weight of institutionally managed assets, central banks working globally as a group, collectively, would be in a stronger position than if acting alone.

If interest rates may not be exactly the right tool what action then can be taken? Since the objective is to frame expectations, not raise the cost of borrowing, overall levels of price variation could be monitored, with the aim of keeping within a certain yield-based range. When prices move outside the range, central bank warnings could be given. If these warnings fail, central banks (or financial regulators working with them – see below) could then charge major operators in the market (such as the largest funds, who own the bulk of the securities) to bring prices to more stable levels, including by limiting turnover or selling stocks. Eventually this kind of operation could become self-policing, once the historical data backing the reference ranges for prices become generally appreciated. Individual stocks showing exceptional promise might still rise in price compared to the others – but not entire markets or classes of stock.

If it is objected that this is an unjustifiable intrusion into the freedom of the market it could be pointed out that central banks and regulatory authorities already have to take action to stop asset price collapses. This occurred in 1987, after the US stock market crash (when the Federal Reserve flooded the markets with liquidity and intermediaries were persuaded to make large buy orders to stabilise the market) and during the 2008 financial crisis (when short-selling was prohibited). The thesis of the recent biography of Alan Greenspan (*The Man Who Knew*, 2016) is that the Chairman of the Federal Reserve in the period 1987 to 2006 was perfectly aware of the dangers of asset price instability (this is what he "knew"), and had written and spoken on the subject (for example, a paper in 1959 on stock price instability, and a speech in 1996 warning of "irrational exuberance" unduly escalating asset values); but as a matter of practical politics concentrated on maintaining US consumer price stability, as a more easily achievable objective.[17]

It could also be pointed out that the ultimate objective would be to stabilise expectations *before* they become prices. Unlike in the real economy, the cost of production does not provide a basic check, or control, on prices; and also, unlike in the real economy, expectations are insufficiently tested when they become part of a "conventional basis of valuation".

For capital assets in the shape of property, or real estate, a similar approach might be taken. A surprisingly high share of bank credit in the developed world is devoted to the financing, or refinancing, of property, rather than (say) the creation of new capital investment by companies. Across the developed countries the average figure approached 60% by 2007 (rising from 35% in 1970); in the UK 65% of all bank lending was devoted to residential mortgages by 2012, and a further 14% for commercial real estate (so making 79% in total).[18] The injection of excessive bank credit into the market for a limited supply of the stock of these types of capital assets is invariably problematic, leading to property price bubbles and crashes. It is noteworthy that this is usually a collective phenomenon: ostensibly competing with one another, banks, through a "conventional basis of valuation", can outbid one another in offering credit to a similar popular type of asset, sometimes eroding creditworthiness standards, causing the price to rise to unsustainable levels, until the supply of credit diminishes (as one day it must) and the price collapses.

If it is impossible for banks, collectively or individually, to resist the pressure to over-lend against an appreciating property asset, a solution is to ensure that the price of such assets remains relatively stable. But central bank countermeasures through interest rates do not appear to be the right tool: property price bubbles can arise during a period of low inflation in the real economy (as in the period before the 2008 financial crisis, otherwise known as the "great moderation"), and so raising interest rates would have a disproportionate effect on the rest of the economy.

Action to influence expectations could, however, be taken. Again, the yardstick would be the extent to which prices depart from the long-term yields of the property in question, to be established on the basis of historic data. As Keynes noted in the *General Theory*, in the case of buildings it is often possible to transfer investor risk by means of long-term contracts with occupiers. Logically, therefore, there should be little reason for radical price shifts, or price instability. In the UK, encouraged by the Bank of England, a cross-industry real estate finance group produced in 2014 the report *A Vision for Real Estate Finance in the UK* (sub-title: *Recommendations for reducing the risk of damage to the financial system from the next commercial real estate crash*) suggesting that long-term value measures should be established for commercial real estate as collateral against bank loans, to be based on the (relatively stable) sustainable cash flows arising from rental income.[19] For central banks, then, property price instability could be judged as the extent to which prices depart from historic yields, measured in ways such as this. In addition to warnings to the market, central banks also have more direct targeted means of controlling commercial banks, including by setting higher reserve requirements to restrict excessive credit creation.

A useful distinction might be made at this point between the creation of credit by banks for completely new capital assets, and the creation of credit for purchasing or refinancing existing capital assets, which comprises most property lending. The creation of credit for new capital assets (or investment) appears unlikely to lead to an asset price bubble, given the dispersed nature of the investment opportunities, and in the case of property the limited space for new construction. It is lending against the stock of existing assets which is usually problematic. It may be possible, then, to restrict lending against existing assets, if the price of the latter has become unstable, and to permit it to continue (or indeed to encourage it) in relation to new investment. (We will return to this point, and the network nature of banking, in the next chapter.) If it is objected that credit-induced property bubbles are hard to detect in their formation, yardsticks of historical yield may provide the answer. And, since central banks already do monitor commercial banks actively, they need to listen carefully to detect the seductive sound of music when it calls commercial banks to come and dance at the asset price ball.

The special case of currencies

Currencies differ from capital assets in not having an underlying yield. Nonetheless, currencies, like other financial prices, are also subject to speculative forces, creating fluctuations between them far in excess of any changes in the underlying economic situation of the issuing countries. In Chapter One we saw how the dollar/German mark rate varied by 50% and more in the 1970s and 1980s. Variations of a similar magnitude have occurred in the dollar/Japanese yen rate. As with other financial prices, when momentum effects build up, currency prices can swing erratically.

How much stability is needed? As Paul Volcker has pointed out, a strong, innovative and stable financial system is fundamental to open trade and to the prosperity of all nations. Currencies need not be absolutely fixed, or rigid, but "We should be able, within a broad range, to manage exchange rates among major currencies in a manner that discourages the extreme changes that are inconsistent with orderly adjustment."[20]

If we think in terms of a framework of expectations, we might recall from Chapter Three that few contracts for the sale of current production exceed five years. Relative currency stability over a period of several years would therefore be beneficial to international trade, the more so if adjustments corresponding to changes in underlying economic circumstances take place in an orderly manner.

Currency stability of this nature is absent from the post-Bretton Woods world. (Indeed, it was the inability to achieve an orderly adjustment of the main world currencies against the value of gold which precipitated the end of Bretton Woods in 1971.) But currency stability is not an outlandish, or intellectually indefensible, proposition. On the contrary: periods of strong world growth, in the late 19th and mid-20th centuries, have been associated with gold-backed international currency stability. The present international "non-system" has, experience suggests, rather little to recommend it: lacklustre growth plus a series of international financial crises have come to replace the orderly adjustment of currencies.

It is generally recognised that the main problem with the Bretton Woods system was that it loaded too much responsibility on the US dollar. Other international currencies were fixed against it, and the dollar was fixed against gold, at a rate originally set as long ago as 1934. While this system worked well in the post-war period so long as US prices were stable, and there was sufficient US gold to meet international claims on dollars, it was not designed to cope with rising domestic inflation in the US in the 1960s and a growing surplus of international dollars held outside the US against a limited stock of gold. Although an orderly adjustment of parities, including that between the dollar and gold, might have taken place within the Bretton Woods system in the early 1970s, this was impossible to agree and a suspension of the gold convertibility of the dollar was all that could be achieved. This suspension became permanent and endures to this day.

If international currency stability resting on the shoulders of one national currency alone – even the US dollar – is too much to expect what is the alternative? In fact, there are several technical possibilities, each requiring a degree of co-operation between the major central banks of the world.

First, there is the alternative gold-based system put forward by Keynes himself during the Second World War, before Bretton Woods in 1944. Instead of the dollar, backed by gold, as the centre of the world monetary system, Keynes proposed an international clearing bank operating between national central banks. Accounts in the international clearing bank would be denominated in a form of central bank money, called "bancor" (or bank gold). Gold would form the standard for intra-central bank transactions, but would not otherwise be used. The clearing mechanism would have a policy purpose: to maintain a balance of payments equilibrium between each member country and the rest of the world. To do this, each central bank would be allotted an index-quota in the clearing bank equal to half the sum of its imports and exports on the average of the previous five pre-war years. A mechanism would ensure that, beyond a certain point, member countries which thereafter ran up deficits in the clearing bank would be able to reduce the exchange value of their national currencies by up to 5% in any year; and member countries which maintained surpluses at the clearing bank would be able to increase the exchange value of their national currencies by up to 5% in any year. In this way, managed variations in international exchange rates would correspond to shifts in balance of payments and international trade.[21]

Another method was sketched out by Keynes earlier, in 1930, in his *Treatise on Money*, using a "tabular standard". Here, major central banks around the world would set up between them another central bank (or use the newly created Bank for International Settlements) to handle transactions between them. Gold held by central banks in this system would be managed so that its long-term value remained stable against a "tabular standard", by which Keynes meant a list of the top sixty commodities (standardised foods and raw materials) of world-wide importance, against which a weighted index would be created. In this way, a gold-based international monetary system would be adjustable in the light of a real economy standard, with the policy objective of avoiding either general international inflation (commodity prices rising too fast against the value of gold) or deflation (commodity prices falling too fast against the value of gold – the situation in the world when Keynes was writing in 1929). As in Keynes' later idea of an international clearing bank, gold and "supernational bank money" would remain purely within the system of central banks, which would have a collective responsibility to maintain between them stable, but adjustable, exchange rates.

As an alternative to using gold or a commodity index as the standard for intra-central bank money, Robert Pringle proposes an intriguing new idea in *The Money Trap* (2012). Pringle, chairman and founder of *Central Banking* and former editor of *The Banker*, reviews a number of theoretical suggestions for currency reform since the demise of Bretton Woods, and suggests that the ultimate standard for money could be real capital assets, measured as a fraction of all equity claims traded on recognised exchanges around the world. After a transitional period, during which major international currencies would be managed within an increasingly narrow range, and then fixed, an anchor for them would be agreed with the IMF, such as a basket of commodities or gold (as in the two Keynes proposals, above). But then, at a later stage, this anchor would be replaced by a new unit of account, based on real capital assets, which Pringle names the "ikon".

Pringle's proposal draws on a paper by the German monetary economist Wolfram Engels (*The Optimal Monetary Unit*, 1981).[22] What is appealing is the idea that money should come to be based on the real productive capacity of the world economy, as opposed to an unproductive metal like gold, or internationally traded commodities. As Pringle points out, this has the consequence that money would be like having an equity share in the productive economy, with potentially great social benefits. ("Money would become a claim on the future of the world economy, giving every citizen a stake in it.")[23] And while it might be objected that the prices of equities currently traded on recognised exchanges around the world are excessively volatile, the same could be said of the price of gold (and commodities generally) since the end of Bretton Woods. A policy objective of asset price stability, and an emphasis on long-term yield, is compatible with, and could pave the way to, a real asset-based monetary standard.

Whichever standard or anchor for currency reform comes to be chosen, the basic objective of any regime, as Pringle says, should be "expectational stability".[24] This idea returns us to Keynes (and also Popper) once again. In the face of an uncertain future, the expectations which affect the performance of the world economy should not be allowed to fluctuate more than is warranted by reference to a real economy standard, and it should be a public policy objective to render them as stable as possible.

To achieve currency stability, various technical solutions based on a real economy standard are therefore possible, for which co-operation between the world's major central banks is a prerequisite. But the basis for such co-operation already exists: there is already a long-established intra-central bank international swap network, used in crises. Moving beyond crisis management, and adding stability of currencies, as well as other financial prices, to the existing central bank objective of real economy consumer price stability should involve no intellectual revolution. We should remember that, to this day, even after the end of the Bretton Woods system in 1971, a guiding purpose of the IMF, as set out in Article I of its Articles of Agreement, is to "promote exchange stability, to maintain orderly exchange arrangements among members, and to avoid competitive exchange depreciation."

Whether such a step needs to involve a full-scale "new Bretton Woods", and a new global international currency agreement, remains to be seen. A possible route would be to work towards stability between a few participating central banks, with close trade and economic connections, as the beginning of a process. The economist Robert Mundell has, for example, proposed creating a core of stability between the US dollar, the euro and the Chinese yuan, together representing about 60% of world GDP, to which other economies could link.[25]

Supporting stability

A public policy objective of financial and asset price stability need not be the sole responsibility of central banks. As we shall see in the next chapter, competition policy might play a role too. And we can consider here how financial regulation might help.

We saw in the previous chapter that the core intellectual assumption on which financial regulation in the UK was based was until the 2008 financial crisis the theory of rational and efficient markets. The first proposition of all was that "Market prices are good indicators of rationally evaluated economic value." This intellectual apparatus was swept away by the financial crisis, and has yet to be replaced.

There is, instead, a renewed emphasis on the concept of "financial stability". At a global level, in 2009 the Group of Twenty countries endorsed the post-crisis creation of a Financial Stability Board, replacing the previous Financial Stability Forum, set up in 1999. The Financial Stability Board, established in Switzerland, has a mandate to:

> [promote] international financial stability; it does so by coordinating national financial authorities and international standard-setting bodies as they work toward developing strong regulatory, supervisory and other financial sector policies. It fosters a level playing field by encouraging coherent implementation of these policies across sectors and jurisdictions.
>
> The FSB, working through its members, seeks to strengthen financial systems and increase the stability of international financial markets. The policies developed in the pursuit of this agenda are implemented by jurisdictions and national authorities.[26]

Similar language can be found in the mandate of the UK financial regulator, the Financial Conduct Authority (the post-crisis successor of the Financial Services Authority), which has among its regulatory objectives that of "financial stability", defined as "contributing to the protection and enhancement of the stability of the UK financial system".[27]

Stable financial systems and markets, whether international or national, are certainly desirable. But what is it that renders them unstable? As we have seen, the prices (or values) placed upon income flows from outstanding financial and capital assets are inherently unstable, because they rely too much on expectations of an uncertain future transmitted between market operators relying on a "conventional basis of valuation". Financial systems and markets become unstable because prices in those markets become unstable.

If financial stability were extended to include the promotion of financial and asset price stability, progress might, however, be possible, and the intellectual void created by the collapse of the theory of rational and efficient markets might be filled. Under this approach, financial regulation would become a policy tool to be used among others in support of price stability. If central bank warnings of price instability do not suffice, regulators, on behalf of central banks, could take targeted measures to dampen the collective behaviour which creates instability. A global rule requiring a fiduciary duty to end savers (as recommended by Bogle in the US) might, for example, be applied to large funds when they act as agents and intermediaries for end savers (principals). Other checks on speculative tendencies might be possible, such as prohibitions on conflicts of interest.

As was remarked by Otmar Issing of the European Central Bank in 2002, "Price stability and financial stability both cannot be achieved in a sustainable way one without the other. They tend to mutually reinforce each other in the long run."[28]

Getting from here to there: a role for "Keynesianism"?

We need to revisit, finally, Keynes' comment that the diagnosis of fluctuations of output and employment in the *General Theory* was meant to be definitive, but suggestions for a cure were not, and could be adapted to the particular conditions of the time. We should bear in mind the underlying problem Keynes was addressing: the need to keep up a sufficient level of effective demand in the economy to sustain supply (and therefore output and employment). Of the components of effective demand, Keynes saw investment as being the crucial variable, and its variability is exacerbated by the fluctuating operations of private investment markets.

In this chapter we have suggested that financial and asset price stability, as a goal of public policy, could counter harmful fluctuations in investment markets. In the next chapter we shall see how competition policy might also work to the same end. In the chapter after that we shall go on to consider how, in light of the discussion so far in this book, a new form of capital market could improve the flow of savings into investment.

But there remains an unanswered policy question. "Keynesian" solutions, involving increases in public expenditure to meet a shortfall in private investment after an acute crisis, may have their role to play in the short term, such as after the 2008 crisis (as in the US, with the American Recovery and Reinvestment Act of 2009). But what about the chronic condition of persistent long-term underinvestment in the developed world, under a financial system which fails to transfer savings into a sufficient volume of current investment in new capital assets?

On the one hand, governments cannot ignore a persistent and chronic investment shortfall. If we take the UK as an example, only a small proportion of bank lending is in practice devoted to new capital investment by companies (only 14% in 2012);[29] and so far as equity markets are concerned little new investment capital has been raised in recent decades (prompting John Kay, the author of the 2012 *Kay Review of UK Equity Markets and Long-Term Decision Making*, for the UK Government, to observe "Equity markets today should primarily be seen as means of getting money out of companies rather than means of putting it in").[30] In 2013 the London School of Economics Growth Commission went so far as to describe investment failure as "the UK's fundamental problem". This, remarkably, is despite the UK having an extremely large banking sector (with assets over four times larger than the national economy),[31] and the largest and most sophisticated capital markets in Europe ("the UK is home to one of the most dynamic world centres for financial services, yet the country seems unable to deliver adequate long-term finance for innovation and private investment.").[32] The LSE Growth Commission advocated completely rethinking UK investment planning, with a comprehensive government strategy covering human capital (education), infrastructure and finance for private investment and innovation.

The creation of the publicly-owned British Business Bank in 2012, focusing on improving the supply of loan financing to small and medium sized firms in the UK, has been a modest step forward. But other countries have larger public operators: in Germany the KfW bank, established as long ago as 1948, committed total financing of EUR 79 billion in 2015 alone; in France there is the Caisse des Depots; and in Italy the Cassa Depositi e Prestiti. Across the EU the publicly-owned European Investment Bank lends significant sums (EUR 78 billion in 2015) for large-scale infrastructure and other projects that would not otherwise obtain private finance.

However, the growing level of public debt built up in the developed world in recent decades places limits on what states can now do. Levels of public debt have risen significantly since the end of the disciplines imposed by Bretton Woods, and vast sums expended on supporting the banking system after the 2008 financial crisis. "Keynesian" deficit-financing cannot be a long-term or sustainable solution to chronic demand deficiency.

A long-term solution appears to require a steady and reliable transformation of savings into investment, via private investment markets less devoted to speculation. In the meantime, public expenditure plans for investment and private plans for investment might, however, be better synchronised to ensure there is no shortfall and to maximise growth and productivity. A public/private growth strategy, if carried out internationally and on a sufficient scale, might even be combined with a mutual debt reduction plan, as economies gradually come back into balance. Curing the "psychology" of finance would then be part of a global health recovery programme, whose object would be to minimise uncertainty and maximise stability.

Such a recovery programme could take as its starting point the commitments the countries of the world have already signed up to, contained in Article IV, Section 1, of the Articles of Agreement of the IMF. These are as follows:

> Recognizing that the essential purpose of the international monetary system is to provide a framework that facilitates the exchange of goods, services and capital among countries, and that sustains sound economic growth, and that a principal objective is the continuing development of the orderly underlying conditions that are necessary for financial and economic stability, each member undertakes to collaborate with the Fund and other members to assure orderly exchange arrangements and to promote a stable system of exchange rates. In particular, each member shall:
>
> (i) endeavor to direct its economic and financial policies toward the objective of fostering orderly economic growth with reasonable price stability, with due regard to its circumstances;
> (ii) seek to promote stability by fostering orderly underlying economic and financial conditions and a monetary system that does not tend to produce erratic disruptions;

(iii) avoid manipulating exchange rates or the international monetary system in order to prevent effective balance of payments adjustment or to gain an unfair competitive advantage over other members; and
(iv) follow exchange policies compatible with the undertakings under this Section.

A "new Bretton Woods" might, paradoxically, begin by breathing life back into the old Bretton Woods, and finding new ways to animate words that have already been agreed.

Notes

1 Minsky H, "Uncertainty and the Institutional Structure of Capitalist Economies", 1996, *Working Paper No.155*, Jerome Levy Economics Institute of Bard College.
2 Remarks by Paul A Volcker at the Annual Meeting of the Bretton Woods Committee, 2014, Washington, "A New Bretton Woods???".
3 In de Larosière J, *Cinquante ans de crises financières*, 2016, Paris, Odile Jacob, page 76.
4 Keynes JM, "The General Theory of Employment", 1937, Skidelsky R (Ed.), *The Essential Keynes*, 2015, London, Penguin, page 266.
5 Roosa R, "Economic Instability and Flexible Exchange Rates", *World Money and National Policies*, 1983, New York, Group of Thirty.
6 "Citigroup chief stays bullish on buy-outs", *Financial Times*, 9 July 2007.
7 Keynes JM, *The General Theory of Employment, Interest and Money*, 1936, London, Macmillan, page 315.
8 Minsky H, *John Maynard Keynes*, 1975, 2008, New York, McGraw-Hill, page 127.
9 *The General Theory of Employment, Interest and Money*, page 320.
10 "The General Theory of Employment".
11 Bogle J, *The Clash of the Cultures*, 2012, Hoboken, New Jersey, John Wiley and Sons, page 80.
12 Woolley P and Vayanos D, "Taming the Finance Monster", 2012, *Central Banking Journal*, December: pages 57–62.
13 Available at "A Vision for Real Estate Finance in the UK", 2014, The Investment Property Forum (www.ipf.org.uk).
14 Smithers A, *The Road to Recovery*, 2013, Chichester, John Wiley and Sons, page 232.
15 *The General Theory of Employment, Interest and Money*.
16 Piketty T, *Capital in the Twenty-First Century*, 2014, Cambridge, Massachusetts, Belknap, page 303.
17 Mallaby S, *The Man Who Knew: The Life and Times of Alan Greenspan*, 2016, London, Bloomsbury.
18 Turner A, *Between Debt and the Devil*, Oxford, Princeton University Press, pages 63 and 67.
19 "A Vision for Real Estate Finance in the UK".
20 Remarks by Volcker: "A New Bretton Woods???".
21 Keynes JM, "Proposals for an International Currency Union", Skidelsky R (Ed.), *The Essential Keynes*, 2015, London, Penguin, page 437.
22 Engels W, *The Optimal Monetary Unit*, 1981, Frankfurt, Campus Verlag.
23 Pringle R, *The Money Trap*, 2012, 2014, Basingstoke, Palgrave Macmillan, page 279.
24 *The Money Trap*, page 280.
25 Letter by Robert Mundell of 20 April 2017 to the Kemp Forum on Exchange Rates and the Dollar (www.jackkempfoundation.org).

26 From the website of the Financial Stability Board (Our Mandate).
27 Section 3A, *Financial Services and Markets Act 2000*.
28 Lessing O, "Why Stable Prices and Stable Markets Are Important and How They Fit Together", speech 2002, European Central Bank, Frankfurt.
29 *Between Debt and the Devil*, page 63.
30 Department for Business, Innovation & Skills, *The Kay Review of UK Equity Markets and Long-Term Decision Making*, 2012 (www.gov.uk).
31 Bush O, Knott S and Peacock C, "Why Is the UK Banking System So Big and Is That A Problem?", 2014, *Bank of England Quarterly Bulletin, Q4*.
32 *Investing for Prosperity: Skills, Infrastructure and Innovation*, Report of the London School of Economics Growth Commission, 2013 (www.lse.ac.uk).

7 Competition policy

How might competition policy support an objective of greater asset and financial price stability? It is true that in general terms, as once pointed out by former European Competition Commissioner Mario Monti, both monetary policy and competition policy are overseen by independent authorities in Europe, and both serve, in different ways, the same objective of price stability.[1]

However, as we saw in Chapter Two, competition policy tends in practice to focus on real economy firms engaged in selling their current output (in the form of goods and services) from the existing stock of capital investments, with the aim of ensuring that market prices are not distorted by firms' own anti-competitive behaviour. Unlike the long-term expectations which relate to new capital investment, expectations here are short-term, and the price mechanism between sellers and buyers acts as the trial and error method for testing them. Competition policy ensures that competing producers (sellers) cannot coordinate expectations of their own sales prices, or fix them through cartels.

The roots of today's competition policy lie in heavy industry. In Europe, the origins of competition policy can be traced back to the European Coal and Steel Community Treaty of 1951, and the need to put in place mechanisms to ensure competitive conditions as coal and steel markets were internationalised in the post-war period. These became the basis for competition policy in the wider common market as extended to all other goods and services, set up by the Treaty of Rome in 1957, with an object (among others) of increasing the division of labour (Adam Smith's phrase) in the European economy.[2] In the US, "antitrust" law dates back even earlier, to the late nineteenth century, and was aimed originally at breaking up the concentration of control of large industries (through trusts). It was estimated that in 1904 some 318 trusts controlled two-fifths of US manufacturing assets.[3] The landmark case was the breakup of Standard Oil in 1911.

Competition policy in Europe (and also in many countries around the world) routinely prohibits anti-competitive agreements and concerted practices between firms of any nature, in particular the fixing of prices in the form of cartels; and the abuse of their position by firms which are dominant in their market. Over the years these prohibitions have come to be applied in virtually all sectors of the economy, including financial services. A cartel of Austrian banks, covering virtually all banking services and products across the country, was found to breach EU competition law in 2002; and in 2016 a cartel of international banks involved in euro interest rate derivatives met the same fate, and was fined almost half a billion euros.

Nonetheless, there is distinct unease about how far banks and other firms involved in financial services can or should be subject to competitive forces, and exactly how competition policy and law should apply. It has not gone unnoticed that countries with more highly regulated (and less competitive) banking sectors emerged rather better than others from the 2008 financial crisis. In 2011 the OECD reported "Studies exploring the complex interactions between competition and stability in retail and commercial banking come to the ambiguous conclusion that competition can be both good and bad for stability. Policy measures that strike an acceptable balance remain elusive."[4] In the UK, competition policy hardly applied at all to capital markets until 2015 (since, according to the theory of rational and efficient markets, it was assumed to have little or no role to play). Only in 2015 did the financial regulator acquire the power to enforce competition law.

A neat description of the dilemma posed by the effect of competition in banking is given by US judge and antitrust expert Richard Posner, remarking on the position at the height of the financial crisis in 2008, when it appeared to each individual US bank that a 1% probability of failure was a chance worth taking, even though a great many banks were heavily invested in financing residential real estate, so that if that 1% probability materialised the entire system of credit would freeze:

> And so it happened in September 2008. But no single bank, in the highly competitive financial-intermediation industry, could justify to its shareholders reducing its risk-taking (for example by reducing its leverage), and therefore their return on equity, merely because the risks that it and its competitors were taking might precipitate a financial crisis that could in turn usher in a depression, just as a wave of bank insolvencies caused by the bursting of a credit-fed stock bubble had ushered in the Great Depression of the 1930s and a wave of bank insolvencies caused by the bursting of a real estate bubble had ushered in Japan's "lost decade" of the 1990s. There would be only one effect of the bank's altruism – of its willingness to sacrifice profits enabled by a slight risk of bankruptcy that most financial executives would think tolerable, as the risk would be unlikely to materialize for a number of years during which they would be making huge amounts of money: the bank would lose out in competition with its daring competitors.[5]

To the three episodes cited by Posner could be added the credit-fuelled Latin American debt crisis of the 1980s (another "lost decade"); the credit-fuelled Nordic debt crisis of the early 1990s; and the credit-fuelled euro-zone debt crisis of the twenty-first century. So regular have they become that these episodes are virtually predictable (and banking supervisory experts in Finland, writing in 2001 on lessons to be learnt from the Nordic banking crisis, *did* predict the euro-zone debt crisis, suggesting the creation of the euro could mean a substantial internationalisation of banking, leading to: (i) the banking system becoming more leveraged because assets can be used more efficiently internationally; (ii) increased competition pushing banks into being more aggressive and taking greater risks; and (iii) national supervisors being less alert to problems outside their own country).[6]

In banking it is as if the normal world turns upside down and inside out: in most industries increased competition causes prices to fall; in banking increased competition seems to cause prices to rise. What on earth is going on?

Hearing secret harmonies: the interdependent world of banking

There are several important differences between banks and normal real economy firms. One is the widespread public or state support, through safety nets and guarantees, resulting from the catastrophic effects of earlier banking failures on the rest of society. Another is the relative ease and speed with which banks can expand and contract their balance sheets, including the credit they create.

Also, unlike most other firms, banks are not essentially competing to put goods and services on the market, in the form of current output from existing capital investments. The core functions of banking (deposit-taking and the extension of credit) are as much co-operative as competitive in nature, with relatively slim margins depending on the difference between banks' funding costs (deposits and borrowings) and the return on their assets (loans). Banks operate within a banking system, and no single bank can operate outside it. Most money in a modern economy is "bank money" (that is, money created by the process of deposit-taking and lending and investing of deposits between banks), but it is not money belonging to or issued by any one particular bank.

The collective and systematic nature of the creation of bank money was well described by Keynes in *A Treatise on Money* (1930), where he pointed out that in a hypothetical closed banking system without cash, and using only cheques for payment, there is no limit to the amount of bank money which banks collectively can safely create; but only provided that they move forward in step:

> Every movement forward by an individual bank weakens it, but every such movement by one of its neighbour banks strengthens it; so that if all move forward together, no one is weakened on balance. Thus the behaviour of each bank, though it cannot afford to move more than a step in advance of the others, will be governed by the average behaviour of the banks as a whole – to which average, however, it is able to contribute its quota small or large.[7]

Keynes went on to add that a monetary system of this kind would possess an inherent instability:

> for any event which tended to influence the behaviour of the majority of the banks in the same direction whether backwards or forwards, would meet with no resistance and would be capable of setting up a violent movement of the whole system.

76 *Competition policy*

In practice, actual monetary systems are not generally as bad as this, and checks on their inherent instability have been devised, such as by keeping reserves at the central bank. Nevertheless:

> this tendency towards sympathetic movement on the part of the individual elements within a banking system is always present to a certain extent and has to be reckoned with. Moreover, where the conditions for a 'closed' system are satisfied, as in the case of a country having an inconvertible paper currency or in the case of the world as a whole, the tendency to instability by reason of sympathetic movement is a characteristic of the utmost practical importance.

The interdependent nature of today's banking is reinforced by other measures, such as co-operation between banks over the interconnection and operation of payment systems. The very largest banks in the world are interconnected by the scale of their intra-financial system assets and liabilities, which is one reason why they were designated "global systemically important banks" by the Financial Stability Board in 2012. In the UK, the extremely large banking sector, with (as we saw in the previous chapter) assets over four times larger than the national economy, is dominated not by banks' relations with their own customers, but by a "complex mesh of intra-financial system claims and obligations".[8]

A realistic view of banking would, therefore, start from an acceptance that this is an interdependent and interconnected industry, subject to state support and prone to generating its own instability by what Keynes called "sympathetic movement" within the system. The pre-war UK banking system which Keynes was describing in *A Treatise on Money* was far from competitive ("There is generally an agreement or understanding between the banks as to the rate of interest which they will allow on deposits of a given type or will charge for loans of a given type").[9] In the post-war period from 1945 until the 1970s, it was generally recognised to be a cartel. In Austria, the completely cartelised banking system which fell foul of EU competition law in 2002 had been in existence for several decades, becoming subject to competition law only when Austria joined the European Economic Area in 1994.

If we pause for a moment here, we might recall that in Chapter Two we referred to Hayek's description of the price system as being like a system of telecommunications, transmitting signals containing essential information around the economy, disseminating useful knowledge to individual producers. The "sympathetic movement" which occurs within a banking system is different: another form of signalling, perhaps, but rather less accurate, and closer to the harmonics and echoes that occur when a stringed musical instrument is struck. "Sympathetic movement" would be another way of describing the Citigroup dance phenomenon: "as long as the music is playing, you've got to get up and dance. We're still dancing." And in Hayek's home country of Austria the banks appeared to be particularly fond of the sound of music.

Because of the interdependencies, events which influence the behaviour of a majority of banks in the same direction can cause a flurry of short-term synchronised competition between them, eroding credit standards and promoting risky behaviour, and the over-extension of credit. Often it is new openings internationally, or the deregulation of markets, or new technical possibilities, which provide the trigger. Since a very high proportion of bank lending in the developed world involves financing capital assets in the shape of property, or real estate, short-term competition to inject additional credit can lead to an asset price bubble, which eventually collapses.

A realistic analysis indicates the difficulties in applying standard competition policy to the world of banking, but also suggests the solution. This is to reverse the procedure which normally applies to firms in a market economy and treat banks not as natural competitors with one another, but as parts of a network industry, able to compete up to a point but needing to be subject to a higher level of competition control.

This can be done under the special provisions of European competition law which permit the usual prohibition on anti-competitive agreements and concerted practices between firms to be declared inapplicable where either agreements or concerted practices contribute to "improving the production or distribution of goods or to promoting technical or economic progress, while allowing consumers a fair share of the resulting benefit"; provided that any restrictions on the firms in question do not go further than is needed to attain these objectives, and competition is not eliminated in respect of a substantial part of the products in question.

By reversing the procedure in this way, bank lending of benefit to the real economy, such as the financing of investment in new capital assets ("improving the production or distribution of goods", or "promoting technical or economic progress") could be encouraged, and competition law declared inapplicable to agreements or concerted practices solely for these purposes. Conversely, systemic bank lending which pushes up the price of the stock of existing assets (in the shape of property) would not be so permitted. "Sympathetic movement" which constitutes a concerted practice here could be prohibited as contrary to competition law. Competition policy could, therefore, contribute in this way to a wider public policy of promoting asset and financial price stability.

Capital markets: more echo chambers

How might capital markets best be approached from this same point of view of encouraging price stability? If we think in terms of Keynes' two types of investors, those in the market who attempt to make reasonable estimates of the long-term yield of capital assets ("enterprise") are unlikely to raise competition policy problems, and nor are they the source of price instability.

The trouble comes with the dominance of those who attempt to forecast the psychology of the market ("speculation"); the more so when, under today's system of institutionalised investment, sufficiently large volumes of funds are engaged to cause prices to shift. In conditions of uncertainty, copying the behaviour of the majority in what Keynes called a "conventional basis of valuation" can cause an excess of either buyers or sellers to build up, with no balancing mechanism.

Competition law has no difficulty in dealing with examples of straightforward collusion between competitors (as in the example of the euro interest rate derivatives cartel, mentioned above, and other recent cases of collusion in the global foreign exchange markets). Once it is established that competitors have manipulated a financial price, or even attempted to manipulate a price, a finding of an infringement of competition law is likely to follow, and fines can be imposed based on the economic impact of the behaviour.

The underlying problem is rather more subtle. Since the prices in question in capital markets (such as the stock market) are not based on real economy costs of production, but are just the momentary values placed at any one time on future income flows from existing capital assets, they are more dependent upon the fluctuating collective expectations of buyers and sellers. And as Keynes pointed out in the *General Theory*, the essence of success in such markets is "foreseeing changes in the conventional basis of valuation a short time ahead of the general public".[10] This is done by "anticipating what average opinion expects the average opinion to be".

Once the assumption that such markets are rational and efficient is removed, there is no presumption they will come to equilibrium. That is why a public policy of promoting price stability is desirable. And once a target of price stability is established, price instability arising from behaviour within the market could then become subject to support by competition policy.

How? Closed, interdependent markets, with tightly-knit and predictable buyers and sellers, have already been addressed by competition policy in the real economy, where collective dominance is defined as the relationship of interdependence between the parties of an oligopoly that "encourages them to align their conduct in such a way as to maximise joint profits".[11] Applying these principles to capital markets dominated by (profit-maximising) speculators, rather than long-term investors, should be possible in situations where copying one another creates a situation of interdependence, and as a result an unstable price.

There is, moreover, a link with asset management, which is the industry which actually owns most of the stocks involved.

Asset management

Since Keynes' day, the big shift has been towards institutional control of the investment industry, so it takes the form today described by Minsky as "money manager capitalism". Total assets under management globally have risen to an estimated US$87 trillion by 2014 (about the same size as world GDP), and are projected to grow further in coming decades. Institutional asset management (via mutual, pension and insurance funds) is responsible for the ownership of most stocks, and also most trading of these stocks (selling back and forth). While it is always open to asset managers to take a long-term approach to investment, based on the long-term yields from holding assets (as some certainly do), the dominant strategy remains a speculative one: buying and selling assets over the short term with the aim of anticipating the psychology of the market, and timing purchases or sales to be ahead of the average, or the market as a whole.

There are a number of practical difficulties with this approach. The first is that, with financial investment now an industry run by professionals, it becomes increasingly hard for any one asset manager to have knowledge about the market which is different from the rest, and therefore to "beat the market". As pointed out in 2017 by investment consultant Charles Ellis, the consequence of a huge increase over the last 50 years in trading volumes on the New York Stock Exchange; a substantial increase in investment research; a proliferation of investment professionals; and instant communication of all sorts of information via trading terminals and the internet, is that institutional investors have collectively created a global expert information network that produces "the world's largest, most effective prediction market":

> The only way for active investors to outperform is to discover and exploit pricing errors by other expert professionals, all having the same information at the same time with the same computers and teams of experts having much the same talent and drive.[12]

One might quibble over the expression "prediction market" but the message is clear. There is no more "general public" for professional investors to outguess, as there was in Keynes' day. All that is left are the professional investors, whose average opinion is known instantly to everyone.

The second difficulty is that this is not a costless exercise. A market study into asset management by the UK Financial Conduct Authority indicated in 2016 that the average annual disclosed fee for actively managed equity funds for UK investors is 0.9% of assets under management; to which should be added transaction costs when assets are bought and sold (which they are, frequently).[13] (As we saw in Chapter Four, Woolley suggests that end-values of pension funds can be reduced by around 30% by these trading activities.)

A third difficulty is that, if anticipating what average opinion expects average opinion to be produces (not surprisingly) an average opinion, why then not simplify the exercise radically by tracking an index of the entire market, which comes to much the same thing? This is the logic behind the much cheaper passive form of investing, as pioneered by Bogle in 1976, which we looked at in Chapter Four. According to some estimates, passive investing may come to constitute half of all asset management within a few years.

A fourth difficulty is that asset management is an agency business, and the assets being managed do not (usually) belong to the manager, but to someone else. The largest pools of savings (pension funds, insurance funds, mutual funds, and also sovereign wealth funds) are collections of savings belonging to individual end savers, not asset managers. Now, as pointed out again by Woolley and colleagues at the London School of Economics, it is not in the interests of savings funds with their own long-term liabilities to end savers (such as pension funds) to engage in a strategy of short-term, market-timing behaviour. What is instead required is a long-term strategy of predictable returns – or, in other words, making reasonable estimates of the long-term yields of capital assets.

It is here we can perhaps also see a role for competition policy. While a few individual end savers may be able to choose how to invest their savings, and whether to take a speculative or long-term view (or, for example, to opt for a passive index fund) the vast majority do not, and delegate responsibility to those who manage the collective savings pool on their behalf. They have no effective choice (and would lack the specialist knowledge of their investment options to exercise it).

Competition policy could, therefore, address the extent to which asset managers provide value for money for captive end savers. This goes beyond fees and costs charged for managed funds: it includes the actual returns to end savers over the relevant life time of the savings vehicle (or the liabilities to end savers of the fund in question). Asset managers compete to attract funds to manage, and have an incentive to grow ever bigger since their remuneration is based on volumes of funds managed. In most industries large volume implies economies of scale, and therefore better goods or services to consumers or purchasers. Is this true in the vast industry of asset management? This is a question to be pursued following the 2016 market study by the FCA.

An industry where the present roles come to be reversed appears more conducive to price stability and also of more benefit to savers: in other words, a market dominated by those making reasonable estimates of the long-term yield of capital assets (or "enterprise") and with those attempting to forecast the psychology of the market (or "speculation") reduced to a secondary role, where they "may do no harm as bubbles on a steady stream of enterprise", as Keynes put it – and one not to be exercised with what (as Adam Smith said) is *"other people's money"*.[14]

The globalisation of competition policy

As we saw in Chapter Two, competition policy has developed gradually over many decades. In the pre-war period some even had the hope that international co-operation between firms, including cartels, would foster peaceful international relations. This did not happen, and the approach changed in the post-war period, with the emphasis on prohibiting firm-to-firm agreements on prices, in the form of cartels; and erecting instead networks of public competition authorities, starting with the developed market economies on both sides of the Atlantic and today covering all the major economies. Prices for the current output of firms remain independently set, and expectations of prices for that output are tested against buyers' willingness to pay. International cartels are still frequently attempted by firms, but also frequently punished through severe fines, related to the economic damage caused.

Globalisation has now extended from trade in goods and services (current output) to flows of finance. By the twenty-first century the US Treasury was estimating that changes in investment positions of institutional money managers meant that "some multiple" of an estimated US$14 trillion of holdings of foreign financial assets was moving across the foreign exchanges each year – which would be much more than WTO estimates of total world exports of merchandise (US$11.8 trillion in 2006).[15]

But financial and asset prices affected by these flows of finance behave differently from prices for current output. Starting with the fluctuations in currencies set in motion by the ending of the Bretton Woods system in the 1970s, international financial and asset prices have come to follow trajectories determined less by underlying economic reality and more by expectations shared between operators in financial markets, pursuing a *"conventional basis of valuation"*.

There is a handy short history of developments by John Authers, the senior investment commentator of the *Financial Times*, in *The Fearful Rise of Markets* (2010). Authers recounts a sequence of fateful steps in this "fearful rise", including the launch of "emerging markets" as an investment idea in the 1980s, resulting in synchronised movements in developed and emerging market equity indexes over the following decades (and, bizarrely, almost complete correlations between movements in the otherwise unrelated Korean and Hungarian equity markets); the development of commodities as an investment "asset class" in the twenty-first century, resulting in previously unrelated financial prices (like Latin American stocks and a commodity index, and the US dollar/euro exchange rate and the price of oil) becoming correlated with one another; and minute-by-minute co-movements of the S&P 500 (the main index of the US stock market) and the US dollar/Japanese yen exchange rate in March 2007, in response to a surprise 9% fall on the Shanghai stock exchange. As Authers says: "As they should have nothing in common, this implies that neither market is being priced efficiently. Instead, these entangled markets are driven by the same investors, using the same flood of speculative money."[16]

For Authers, October 2008 was a watershed, when at the height of the financial crisis virtually all world stock markets lost a fifth of their value in a week, and 16 different asset classes (government and corporate debt, equities, loans and commodities from around the world) fell in value together:

> This collapse was the ultimate proof that different asset classes, many of which had only opened to investors after financial innovations of the last decade, had come to reinforce one another. The value of each was not contingent on real world conditions as much as valuations in other markets. This was the ultimate consequence of the herd-like behaviour that the investment industry had encouraged for decades; the herd finally stomped over all of the world's markets.[17]

Since the financial crisis, financial asset prices have continued to be closely correlated with one another. As observed by the Chief Economist of the Bank of England in 2015:

> One striking feature of the past few years has been the extremely high correlations among asset prices globally, in particular among advanced economies. This is true of both "safe" rates of return on government assets and "risky" rates of return on private assets. In either case, correlations are extremely high, hovering around 0.9.[18]

82 Competition policy

The correlations to which Haldane referred to were equity prices in the US, UK and euro areas, and also yields on ten-year government bonds in the US, Germany and France. (A correlation of 1 would mean they are the same.) Synchronised markets, driven by the same investors, have persisted years after the financial crisis.

Globalisation in finance is today perhaps somewhere near the position globalisation in the real economy was in the pre-war period: destabilising if left to its own devices. There exists now the closed and unstable system for banking which Keynes warned of "in the case of the world as a whole". The supposition that free movement of capital will lead to the efficient allocation of resources has proved incorrect. A distinction needs to be made between finance devoted to new investment (that is, the creation of new capital assets) and finance devoted to existing investment (that is, buying and selling rights to existing capital assets). Nearly all financial activity is focused on the latter, and as these rights are transferred back and forth across financial markets they become interchangeable with rights to other capital assets, so causing prices to link and rise and fall together. The consequence is that the stock of productive capital of the world, which is an objectively fixed sum, is permanently shifting in value, as if it were a mirage. At the same time, the output of that stock (goods and services) is subject to competition rules to ensure it is priced correctly, so promoting price stability.

If we think back to Hayek's description of the price system as a system of telecommunications, it means a mechanism for sending signals around the economy, transmitting useful and practical "knowledge of the particular circumstances of time and place". In this way, not only a division of labour but also a co-ordinated utilisation of resources based on divided knowledge becomes possible. Mispricing of capital assets on a global scale indicates that this kind of useful and practical knowledge is not being transmitted around the globe.

We should also recall Keynes. In a situation of uncertainty, short-term expectations for current output can be checked and corrected by the operation of the price mechanism; but the expectations governing additions to the existing stock of capital equipment (or investment) are long-term. These long-term expectations are influenced by the current market valuations of already existing capital assets – today increasingly prone to give off correlated and misleading signals. Thus, expectations remain volatile, and so does global investment.

Competition policy might help address this problem. Among the prohibitions under competition law are any agreements or concerted practices which have either the object or the effect of preventing, restricting or distorting competition, including those which "limit or control production, markets, technical development or investment".[19] For competition policy to move beyond the first price system in the market economy (for current output) to look into the operation of the second price system (valuing income flows from outstanding financial and capital assets) may appear to some a radical step – or really no more than catching up with a process of globalisation that has already been under way for several decades.

To do so would be consistent with a policy of promoting asset and financial price stability; and also the "continuing development of the orderly underlying conditions that are necessary for financial and economic stability" (IMF Article IV, Section 1), to which IMF members are already committed. Aggregate price stability should make individual price signals more meaningful – as in the real economy. And aggregate price stability should then allow a higher proportion of financial investment to be based on yield, as a measure of value beyond price.

Improvements in the operation of capital markets may also help. This will be the subject of the next chapter.

Notes

1 Monti M, "Competition Policy and Monetary Policy: A Comparative Perspective", 2006, Per Jacobsson Foundation lecture, Bank for International Settlements.
2 *Comité Intergouvernemental Créé par la Conférence de Messine, Rapport des Chefs de Délégation aux Ministres des Affaires Etrangères*, Bruxelles, 21 April 1956, Archives nationales, Paris, Brochures doc Mae 120 (*Spaak Report*, translation by the author).
3 Johnson S and Kwak J, *13 Bankers*, 2010, New York, Pantheon Books, page 24.
4 *Bank Competition and Financial Stability*, 2011, Paris, OECD, page 6.
5 Posner R, *A Failure of Capitalism*, 2009, Cambridge, Massachusetts, Harvard University Press, page 322.
6 Mayes D, Halme L and Liuksila A, *Improving Banking Supervision*, 2001, Basingstoke, Palgrave, page 7.
7 Keynes JM, *A Treatise on Money (Vol I, The Pure Theory of Money)*, 1930, 2013, Cambridge, Cambridge University Press, page 23.
8 Turner A, "What Do Banks Do, What Should They Do and What Public Policies Are Needed to Ensure Best Results for the Real Economy?", speech 2010, Financial Services Authority, London.
9 Keynes JM, *A Treatise on Money* (*Vol II, The Applied Theory of Money*), 1930, 2013, Cambridge, Cambridge University Press, page 253.
10 Keynes JM, *The General Theory of Employment, Interest and Money*, 1936, London, Macmillan, page 154.
11 Case T-102/96 Gencor v Commission, 1999, 4 *Common Market Law Review*, page 971.
12 Ellis C, "Technology and Low Returns: The End for Active Investing?" *Financial Times*, 21 January 2017.
13 *Asset Management Market Study – Interim Report*, 2016, Financial Conduct Authority.
14 And the title of Kay J, *Other People's Money*, 2015, London, Profile Books.
15 *US Treasury Report to Congress on International Economic and Exchange Rate Policies*, 2007, Appendix 1: Cross Border Capital Flows and Foreign Exchange Market Activities.
16 Authers J, *The Fearful Rise of Markets*, 2010, Harlow, Financial Times Prentice Hall, page 2.
17 *The Fearful Rise of Markets*, page 153.
18 Haldane A, "On Microscopes and Telescopes", speech 2015, Bank of England.
19 Article 101, 1 (b), *Treaty on the Functioning of the European Union*, OJEU C 326/88, 26.10.2012.

8 A new European capital market

"It is time to query whether the stock markets that consume so much resource and receive so much attention any longer serve an important economic function."

(John Kay)[1]

In a way it is surprising that comparatively little thought has been devoted to the economic purpose of the stock market until well into the twenty-first century. Technical and technological adjustments have been made over the decades, and stock markets have internationalised, proliferated, merged and become subject to competition from other trading platforms, but few have questioned their basic rationale, or suggested they need completely rethinking. That the economist John Kay, who in 2012 led an official review for the government of UK equity markets, should do so is striking. Is it possible to rethink the stock market to ensure a better flow of savings into investment?

Origins

Stock markets originated in the need of individuals who had clubbed together to form joint-stock companies, like the East India Company, to sell their holdings to each other. There developed a secondary market for shares in joint-stock companies, which at first in the eighteenth century in the UK were traded in coffee houses in London but by 1773 were centralised in one site. Similar developments took place in Amsterdam, New York and Paris. By 1801, the London Stock Exchange was established in broadly its current form. The antiquity of these early arrangements (with roots predating the French Revolution and American Independence) is to be noted, as is the fact that all that was actually being exchanged was an existing ownership right in an existing company.

Nineteenth century legislative reforms in the UK made the incorporation of companies easier; established the principle of a company having its own legal identity; and limited the liability of investors to the amount invested in a company.

The formal separation between ownership and management of business is the starting point of the analysis of Keynes in the *General Theory*, in the 1930s. Keynes pointed out that whereas in former times enterprises were mainly owned by those who undertook them or by their friends and associates, separate ownership and management, and the development of organised investment markets, introduced a new factor of great importance "which sometimes facilitates investment but sometimes adds greatly to the instability of the system". The stock exchange allows frequent revaluations of existing investments, and these revaluations exert a "decisive influence" on the rate of current investment. This is because when a company's shares are quoted very high it can raise capital by issuing more shares on favourable terms, which has the same effect as if it could borrow at a low rate of interest. Or, to put it another way, a high quotation for existing equities involves an increase in the marginal efficiency of the corresponding type of capital and therefore has the same effect (since investment depends on a comparison between the marginal efficiency of capital and the rate of interest) as a fall in the rate of interest.

However, despite the importance of these revaluations of existing investments, several factors make the operation of the system precarious. First, precisely because ownership of the stock of equity in the community is dispersed among persons who do not manage and have no special knowledge of the business in question, there is a serious decline in the real knowledge of the value of investments by those who buy or own them. Second, ephemeral and insignificant day-to-day fluctuations in profits have an excessive, and indeed absurd, influence on the market. Third, the market is subject to waves of optimistic and pessimistic sentiment, with no solid basis for a reasonable calculation, when a conventional valuation is established as the outcome of the "mass psychology of a large number of ignorant individuals". Fourth, competition between expert professional investors is not usually to correct the vagaries of the ignorant individual investor left to himself, but rather to foresee changes in the conventional basis of valuation a short time ahead of the general public. Thus the professional investor is forced to concern himself with the anticipation of impending changes, "in the news or in the atmosphere", of the kind by which experience shows that the mass psychology of the market is most influenced.

As the organisation of investment markets improves, so does the risk increase of the predominance of speculation (the activity of forecasting the psychology of the market) over enterprise (the activity of forecasting the prospective yield of assets over their whole life). Keynes viewed the largest investment markets of New York as being under an "enormous" influence of speculation, noting it was said that when Wall Street is active, at least half of the purchases or sales of investments are entered upon with an intention on the part of the speculator to reverse them the same day. These tendencies are, moreover, the almost inevitable outcomes of having successfully organised liquid investment markets.

Keynes' antipathy towards speculators was not confined to the *General Theory*. In a speech in 1938 he added that speculative markets "are governed by doubt rather than by conviction, by fear more than by forecast, by memories of last time and not by foreknowledge of next time. The level of stock exchange prices does not mean that investors know, it means that they do not know."[2]

This takes further Keynes' observation, above, that the dispersed ownership of stock among many investors entails a serious decline in knowledge of the value of investments. Matters are not helped when values are set, conventionally, by "a large number of ignorant individuals". The diminished level of knowledge when ownership and management of business are separated is not corrected by the speculative transactions taking place in liquid investment markets. It is not as if dispersed knowledge is reassembled and brought back together (as in Hayek's telecommunications system for producer prices in the real economy). Aggregate knowledge levels remain poor, and emotions and mass psychology can easily prevail when setting prices. Investors do not "know".

We can view this also from a Popperian trial and error (and knowledge-creation) perspective. Expectations of producer prices in the real economy can be checked and corrected by the short-term trial and error process of the price mechanism. But expectations of the value of investments are not checked and corrected but multiply and feed off each other in speculative markets. The underlying capital stock of businesses (the ultimate source of the relevant knowledge) remains little changed: but the unchecked expectations of speculators, lacking a solid basis of knowledge, can veer wildly.

Keynes' concern was not merely academic. The risks of an unstable system had already been vividly demonstrated in the Wall Street crash of 1929, when there was (in Keynesian terminology) a collapse in the marginal efficiency of capital, with disillusion falling upon an over-optimistic and over-bought market "with catastrophic force". The result was an "appalling collapse" in net capital formation in the US after 1929, falling in 1932 to a figure 95% below the average for the period 1925–29.

The Wall Street crash, and the Depression, hang over the *General Theory* – as they hung over all economic and political developments in the US and Europe in the highly unstable period leading up to the outbreak of the Second World War.

The post-war period

As we have already seen, the post-war period has been marked by a major shift towards institutionalised savings and investment, accentuating further the separation between ownership and management of companies. Ownership of shares has come to be held by pools of collective savings, rather than by individual investors, or by company management.

On the whole this has not, however, rendered the system more stable, or diminished the influence of speculation. Backed by the theory of efficient markets, the emphasis instead has been on making the exchange of shares easier, quicker and cheaper. Daily trading volumes have massively increased, from about 2 million shares per day in the US in the 1950s to some 8.5 billion per day in recent decades.

In 1975, following a steady rise in trading by institutions on the New York Stock Exchange (to over half of the volume by 1969) there came the abolition, on "May Day", of all fixed commission rates for brokerage, the consequence of which was that large institutional investors could negotiate better fees for transactions than small investors. The counterpart in the UK was "Big Bang" in 1986, when fixed stock exchange commissions were also abolished, and the business model of brokers on the stock exchange shifted from one of agency, handling orders on behalf of investor customers, to one of "market making" (offering as a principal to buy and sell securities at all times).

Market making is an inherently more risky business, and it is instructive to note that none of the independent firms operating on the UK stock exchange at the time of Big Bang has remained independent. In the recent words of economist Andrew Smithers:

> Today market making is mainly confined to banks and is an important part of their activities. This may, without exaggeration, be described as a kind of doomsday machine in which regular collapses are highly likely and almost inevitable and in which each collapse is likely to be larger than the last. This is clearly a foolish arrangement and, to make it even more absurd, it is one that is currently subsidised by taxpayers.[3]

In October 1987 there occurred a further stock market crash in New York (the largest one-day drop in history – greater than any one-day drop in 1929). A survey of almost 1,000 US investors conducted immediately afterwards by US economist Robert Shiller provided further evidence of the circularity of the price-setting process. No one news story or external event was thought by investors to be immediately responsible, but feedback channels within the market, with investors reacting to one another, appeared to them the main cause of price declines feeding into further price declines. Most investors interpreted the crash as due to the psychology of "other investors". Shiller commented that investors had expectations before the 1987 crash that something like a 1929 crash was a possibility, and comparisons with 1929 were part of this phenomenon:

> It would be wrong to think that the crash could be understood without reference to the expectations engendered by this historical comparison. In a sense many people were playing out an event again that they knew well.[4]

The role of expectations in price setting is once again evident. Lacking an anchoring, investors do not "know" and end up reacting to one another when setting prices. And "fear" and "memories of last time" can set the pace.

In this case, memories of 1929 also remained with the US authorities, who flooded the markets with liquidity and persuaded investors to make large buy orders to prop up the stock market. There was minimal long-term damage to the real economy, and no generalised collapse in the marginal efficiency of capital.

Since the 1980s, with higher volumes of trading between institutions as the backdrop, venues for exchanging stocks have proliferated and the speed of transactions has accelerated. By 2011 the UK competition authorities reported there were in fact four exchanges accounting for most trading of UK equities, with the traditional London Stock Exchange now responsible for less than half and three "multilateral trading facilities" most of the rest. In the US, there were by the twenty-first century some thirteen exchanges and fifty "dark pools" (private trading venues used by institutional investors). High frequency trading, where holding periods range from between one day to less than a second, accounted for between two-thirds and three-quarters of US equity market volume by turnover by 2011. And in May 2010 there occurred yet another sudden stock market crash, the so-called "Flash Crash", when the US Dow Jones experienced its largest ever intraday fall, losing US$1 trillion of market value in the space of about half an hour, and with the prices of established companies departing completely from reality, before in most cases bouncing back again the same day.

Compared to the extraordinary volumes and speed of buying and selling existing equities, the amount of new capital actually raised by companies by issuing shares on the stock exchange has been rather more modest. In the US Bogle puts the figure at an average of US$250 billion a year; less than 1% of the value of annual trading in stocks. In the UK, as we saw in Chapter Six, a remarkable finding of John Kay, in his official 2012 review of UK equity markets, was that equity markets have not actually been an important source of capital for new investment in British companies for many years. Instead, since in the previous decade companies had raised less finance through issuing new shares than they had bought shares for cash for takeovers and buy-backs, "Equity markets today should primarily be seen as a means of getting money out of companies rather than a means of putting it in."

In the UK the stock market therefore now appears to do little to provide investment finance for companies to create new capital assets; and, as we have already seen, the banking sector appears to do little either, with most (79%) of bank credit devoted either to residential or commercial property. The Kay review noted a marked decline in business investment in the UK in the decade 2000 to 2010; and, indeed, the long-term picture in the post-war period has been one of diminishing investment (with the exception of new buildings and structures), prompting the London School of Economics Growth Commission to report in 2013 that investment failure is "the UK's fundamental problem".[5]

Whatever the economic functions of today's stock market, facilitating investment is not very high on the list.

After the financial crisis

Although the crash of 1987 had little impact on the real economy, the financial crisis of 2008 did. In 2013 the European Investment Bank reported that gross fixed investment across the EU was some 17% below its peak in 2008. This is nothing like as catastrophic as the almost total collapse in investment in the US in the 1930s, but underscores the need to boost investment levels across Europe.

Banks have traditionally been the source of most finance for business in Europe. But since the financial crisis largely manifested itself in Europe as a banking crisis, several factors have constrained the ability of banks to step up lending. These include the need to repair their own damaged balance sheets; the impact of higher regulatory capital requirements; and the maintenance by central banks of extremely low (almost zero) interest rates, making it hard for banks to lend profitably, with a reasonable spread between funding costs (deposits and borrowings) and the return on their assets (loans to businesses).

It is understandable that the European authorities have been keen to encourage the development of capital market finance, both to make up for the post-crash shortfall in investment and to boost long-term growth levels in Europe. But in doing so there are valuable lessons which can be learnt from those capital markets which have been in existence the longest, and developed the furthest. There is no particular reason to duplicate their worst features.

In the case of the UK, the almost total absence of additional capital raised on the stock market for business investment should give pause for thought. If the object of the exercise is to boost investment, productivity, research and development and growth, the traditional UK model cannot be adopted without adjustment.

In the case of the US, it is true there are enormous capital markets when measured in terms like volume of turnover, but measured in terms of additional capital raised for business an average annual figure of US$250 billion is more modest (about 60% more than, say, combined annual lending of the two institutions the German KfW bank (EUR 79 billion) and the European Investment Bank (EUR 78 billion) in 2015). Moreover, the speculative nature of the US stock market has already been mentioned. Bogle, founder of the largest mutual fund in the US (and proponent of low-cost, passive investing based on tracking a simple US stock market index), has cited Keynes' comments on the role of speculation in US investment markets in the 1930s, adding that the same situation prevails today, *"only far more strongly"*.[6] Achieving volumes of trading on a US scale would be impossible in Europe in the short term; and nor does it seem necessary or wise to rebuild Wall Street across the Atlantic and duplicate the destabilising element of speculation.

How then might things be improved?

Towards a new European capital market

Although there are numerous stock markets in Europe, competing for volumes of short-term trading in securities by financial intermediaries, there exists no long-term capital market, on a pan-European scale, expressly designed to match the investment needs of European companies, on the one hand, and savers, on the other.

How might creating one be approached? A starting point would be the recognition that institutional savings are the dominant players in today's financial investment. When Minsky coined the phrase "money manager capitalism" in 1996 to describe the ownership of most financial instruments by mutual and pension funds, there were something like US$11 trillion in pooled and managed savings around the world. By 2006 this figure had reached an estimated US$60 trillion; by 2014 it was an estimated US$87 trillion; and some project it rising to US$100 trillion by 2020.[7]

Dispersed knowledge about the value of companies is not, however, improved by ever more frequent and rapid buying and selling of existing shares by intermediaries on behalf of these institutions. What is required instead is a more effective method of valuing shareholdings over a longer period of time, during which the performance of a company can be measured more meaningfully. We have seen from previous chapters that actual yields of capital assets differ from current financial prices (the fluctuating values placed at any one moment upon future income flows from these assets). This explains Keynes' distinction between speculation and "enterprise", or the activity of forecasting the prospective yield of assets over their whole life.

Yields from investment are, on aggregate, stable over long periods of time, as are yields from well-established companies. Average annual real rates of return on capital appear to hover around the 4–5% mark (and have done since the eighteenth century); and for companies in the US in the 150 years up to 2012 Bogle reports that dividend yields have aggregated at 4.5% annually, with real earnings growth a further 2.5% annually.[8]

Against this background, a new kind of capital market for long-term institutional savings could modify the functions of traditional stock markets, along the following lines. First, the *exchange* function (for buying and selling existing shares in companies) could be adapted to incorporate the idea of long-term yield. To do this, for those companies participating in this capital market, a database could be created of historic previous yields, over as long a period as records are available. (Yields for these purposes can be taken to mean dividends plus earnings growth: and possibly other measures of long-term value, provided a consistent approach is taken.) Since good records of previous performance need to exist, this suggests the larger established European companies would be most suitable. Companies making up the FT Europe 500 (the largest 500 European companies, based on market capitalisation, updated annually) would be examples.

On this basis, in 2015 the first twenty European firms would have been as follows:

Novartis
Nestlé
Roche
Anheuser-Busch Inbev
Royal Dutch Shell
HSBC
Sanofi
Volkswagen
Bayer
Unilever
Total
BP
Novo Nordisk
GlaxoSmithKline
Banco Santander
Daimler
L'Oréal

Inditex
British American Tobacco
Basf

Having created a database of long-term value, large savings institutions which wish to sell or buy large blocks of shares between them (above a certain minimum size) would have an objective basis for direct transactions where holdings are to be retained for the long term. An institutional purchaser who wanted, for example, to bid to obtain a block of shares in a company to be held for the next ten (or twenty) year period would be able to see the yield in the previous ten (or twenty) year period, and the period before that, as far back as records exist. Sellers would have access to the same data. The price of transactions between bidders and sellers would be set in the market, taking account of duration and volume. Intermediaries like market makers would not be necessary. While, of course, there can be no guarantee that previous yields will persist into the future, the evidence is that long-term trends rarely change, and these trends are more predictable than short-term speculative prices. Therefore, the longer the reference period chosen, the more stable the yield.

In this way, the shortfall in knowledge about the value of companies when shareholdings are dispersed could be corrected. Transactions of this nature would be based on objective knowledge of company performance so far, over a long-term period. Expectations of the future value of investments would be more anchored, and less prone to shifts in a volatile "conventional basis of value".

Other short-term stock markets and trading platforms would still exist around Europe, where current prices of many of these companies would still be quoted by intermediaries. It is, however, reasonable to expect that a long-term capital market of this nature would serve to dampen erratic prices in these short-term markets, contributing to the general policy of asset price stability proposed in Chapter Six. In the UK, although companies have not in practice raised significant finance from the stock market, they still remain under the influence of short-term stock market price fluctuations (revaluing old investments). This short-termism extends to company investment decisions, and Smithers has put forward the plausible theory that management incentives and bonuses boosting short-term stock prices have now become a structural factor inhibiting new long-term investment.[9]

Second, the *investment* function in this kind of capital market could differ from existing stock markets. Companies that wished to issue shares to obtain new capital could use it to issue a special or preferential class of shares to long-term institutional investors, to be held for periods of time like ten or twenty years (and not immediately resold, as at present). To do this, incentives to investors might include a commitment to compound dividend payments over a ten or twenty year period. Both companies and institutional investors would be able to draw on the database of previous yields over previous periods of time (plus actual transactions that have taken place via the exchange function). In this way, long-term direct investments of large savings funds in a wide range of companies should become possible, which better match the liabilities of the funds themselves. (If we assume that, on average, the long-term trend is for yields to run in the 4–5% region, the question for investors is how this compares with other investment opportunities, like bonds.) A wide spread of large European companies would help institutional investors diversify their long-term shareholdings, across countries and industries.

The organisation of such a new capital market should not in practice prove excessively difficult. The core functions of the market (exchange and investment) would need to be backed by the creation and maintenance of a database of previous long-term yields of companies. These activities could be undertaken by a private body, of a modest size. Regulation would need to be pan-European but, given the nature of the activities, the absence of intermediaries engaged in the risky business of market making, and the fact that neither capital nor investment funds would be held by the market body, should not be onerous. Participating European companies and institutional investors would need to subscribe to the capital market on terms to be agreed (such as via a fee).

A pan-European scale

Why should such a new capital market be organised on a Europe-wide basis?

First, the size of the funds now pooling savings across the world is so enormous that a large-scale continental operation is justified. Each national market in Europe is relatively small, and in many cases dominated by a small number of large companies. A pan-European approach, including a large number of large companies, covering a continent with a population of 500 million plus, would give institutional investors a new and wide selection of long-term opportunities. We saw in the previous chapter how it is becoming increasingly difficult for active asset managers, pursuing speculative short-term strategies, to differentiate themselves from each other and "beat the market" when everyone has instant access to the same information and opinions. Institutional investors pursuing a different long-term strategy on behalf of their end savers could, instead, invest in a spread of large European companies, allowing them to match the income streams (yields) with their own liabilities to savers.

Second, while savings continue to accumulate in Europe there is very little connection between those savings and investments in real economy companies. As Jacques de Larosière has pointed out, household savings in countries like France, Germany and Italy are structurally high (respectively 15%, 17% and 11% of incomes) and stable, and ensure more than 80% of the financing of their economies. The financial part of these savings is of a precautionary nature, and the majority of funds are placed in savings accounts, insurance and pension funds which are themselves invested in "safe" assets (usually government bonds, with low rates of return).[10] In 2016 euro area insurance companies held EUR 7.3 trillion in assets, and pension funds about EUR 2.4 trillion, and in the UK asset managers about £6.9 trillion in assets, of which £3 trillion was on behalf of UK pension funds and other institutional investors.[11]

But direct holdings of equities by European households are extremely limited, and even those institutions like insurance companies and pension funds which once were significant buyers of equities have been reducing their holdings, under regulatory pressures and benchmarking habits, in favour of bonds. This creates a further problem in that the liabilities of life insurance and pension funds to their own policy holders and beneficiaries can be of a longer duration than the maturity profile of bonds held to meet those obligations. Stress tests of insurance companies in 2013 indicated that in many European countries the duration of assets held was several years shorter than the duration of liabilities (in the case of Germany, assets of ten years against liabilities of twenty years).[12]

There is, therefore, a general need to find a better transmission mechanism to move a higher proportion of savings in Europe into productive investment in real economy companies; and also better and more long-term equity assets to match the liabilities of large savings funds to their end savers. (This problem is already recognised: see, for example, the proposal for a European Savings Account, to be used to fund long-term investments, in the paper "Towards a true European Investment Fund".)[13]

Third, there are wider macroeconomic consequences of cumulative low investment across Europe, as an element of effective demand. The investment shortfall since the financial crisis has already been mentioned, with a 17% drop since the peak in 2008. But low investment and low growth in Europe predate the financial crisis. De Larosière has calculated that, in cumulative terms, from 1998 to 2015 productive investment in the US as a percentage of GDP was 20 points higher than in Germany; corporate debt is significantly higher in France and Germany than in the US; and research and development is higher in the US (at 3% of GDP) than in the euro area (which has a target of reaching 3% by 2020).[14] The UK scores particularly badly, with the lack of investment the UK's "fundamental problem" (above), and research and development levels in 2008 even lower than those of France, Germany and the US.[15]

Some of the shortfall in investment in Europe may be made up through a boost in infrastructure expenditure (in transport, energy, telecommunications and so forth) where there is a recognised need for higher levels of investment (estimated to be EUR 650 billion per annum until 2020). With this aim, the "Juncker Plan" envisages using public European funds to leverage private finance, of which a high proportion would be invested in infrastructure. A new European capital market could add to this initiative; public and private owners of infrastructure assets, with predictable streams of income (yields), could use it to raise new capital from institutional investors. This could be done either through issuing long-term shares in companies themselves (as in the investment function, described above) or, if the database can be extended to include yields from large-scale capital assets in the shape of infrastructure, shares in those capital assets. As with investments in companies, if a consistent method of comparing yields can be established, institutional investors would have a spread of long-term investments to add as assets to match their long-term fund liabilities.

A long-term capital market in Europe might, then, help reverse the current trend whereby large volumes of savings are withdrawn from current consumption, hardly contribute to investment at all and are kept (mostly) by institutions in government debt instruments. The object would be a virtuous circle where a higher proportion of European savings is used for productive investment, there is more equity instead of debt and European companies have recourse to new and wider pools of capital, to improve their productivity and growth.

Retrospective: Europe in the post-war period

It may perhaps be useful to put an initiative like this into context by considering here the course of European economic integration in the light of the two-price market economy analysis adopted in this book (that is, one price system for valuing the current output of goods and services; and another, more volatile, price system for valuing income flows from outstanding financial and capital assets).

The original European Coal and Steel Community, set up by the 1951 Treaty of Paris, was essentially about current output: the object was to place the whole of French and German production of coal and steel under an international authority with membership open to other European countries; and for this authority to have as its purpose the unification of the conditions of production, leading to a gradual extension of effective co-operation in other areas.

The originator of this initiative was Jean Monnet, and the blocked immediate post-war situation he was addressing he described as follows in his Memoirs:

> Germany expanding; German dumping on export markets; a call for the protection of French industry; an end to trade liberalization; the re-establishment of pre-war cartels; perhaps, Eastward outlets for German expansion, a prelude to political agreements; and France back in the old rut of limited, protected production.[16]

The Treaty of Rome in 1957 built on the innovative approach adopted in the Coal and Steel Community to create a common market for all goods and services, going beyond the sectors of coal and steel. In the words of the 1956 Spaak Committee Report, on which the Treaty of Rome was based:

> The object of a common European market must be to create a vast area of common economic policy, constituting a powerful unit of production, and allowing continued expansion, increasing stability, faster growth in living standards and the development of harmonious relations between the states it unites. To attain these objectives, a merging of separate markets is an absolute necessity. This will permit, by the increased division of labour, an elimination of waste of resources and, by increasing the security of supply, a halt to production regardless of cost.[17]

The reference to Adam Smith is clear: the merging of markets was to allow an increased division of labour, and rising living standards, across the whole of western Europe. These objectives suit normal real economy markets, where producer prices are based on costs and expectations are tested through the price mechanism, operating between sellers and buyers. As part of building the common market, strong competition law rules were added to ensure that the price mechanism is not distorted by the behaviour of companies.

The Treaty of Rome also set up the European Investment Bank, whose main purpose was to finance projects of benefit to the common market, drawing on the capital markets to do so. But apart from this, the European Community (later the European Union) had comparatively little centralised public expenditure, with a budget equivalent to only around 1% of EU GDP, and much of this devoted to agricultural support.

The economic expansion foretold in the Spaak Report nonetheless came to pass. Trade boomed in the common market, as did economic growth and average income levels. This expansion continued into the 1960s, with GDP growth of 4.8% a year over the 1960–73 period. But then came the end of the Bretton Woods system in 1971, and the first oil price shock in 1973. Instability, high inflation and low growth ensued. Policy focused on disinflation and exchange rate stability, and the launch of the European Monetary System in 1979 aimed at recreating a Bretton Woods-like region of currency stability. A decade of reasonable success in building a zone of price and currency stability in Europe led to the decision in 1989 to move to a single European currency, and the euro was launched in 1999.

To regain growth, the main European initiative from the 1980s onward has been to relaunch, and improve, the common market through the European single market programme. In the words of the amendment to the Treaty of Rome introduced by the 1987 Single European Act, the object was to create "an area without internal frontiers in which the free movement of goods, persons, services and capital is ensured".

The free movement of capital thus became a policy object, as part of the single market. The assumption was that capital would flow to where it was most needed and that, by removing barriers, capital, like goods and services, would cross borders and so lead to a more efficient allocation of resources.

This may have been making a virtue of necessity. The Treaty of Rome was cautious on capital liberalisation, and for several decades it was limited to capital directly associated with the free movement of goods, services and people. But by the 1980s, and in the post-Bretton Woods world of floating global currencies, controls on capital movements appeared antiquated. For financial services, the objectives were described as follows by the European Commission in 1992:

> The Community is aiming to establish a single market in financial services as part of the wider single European market due to be in place in 1993, allowing banks to offer the full range of their services throughout the entire Community and to set up branches in other Member States as easily as their own, enabling customers to buy insurance providing cover throughout the Twelve on the most reasonable terms, and ensuring that the market for securities and capital is of a size sufficient to meet the financing needs of European industry and to attract investors from all over the world.[18]

When we look into these three types of financial services, insurance appears not fundamentally different from a service in other real economy markets, with little impact on capital assets, or their prices. Creating a market for securities and capital sufficient to meet the financing needs of European industry has, of course, not yet happened (and hence it is the subject of this chapter).

The banking sector has proved particularly problematic, as the traditional source of most finance for European business, and the main source of cross-border capital flows. The interdependent and interconnected nature of banking was described in the previous chapter, where it was suggested a realistic assessment would view individual banks as not so much natural competitors with one another but more parts of a network industry, susceptible to destabilising "sympathetic movement" affecting the banking network as a whole. Despite many initiatives to promote cross-border services since the 1980s, the European retail banking sector was found by the Commission in 2007 (on the eve of the financial crisis) to be still fragmented along national lines, including through banking infrastructure, payment systems and credit registers. This should not really be surprising: the networks and systems which banks operate in, allowing them to accept deposits and lend and invest deposits in other banks (and thus collectively create most of the money in the economy), have developed nationally over many decades, and are not simple to replicate or rationalise from one country to another.

However, "sympathetic movement" in a bank network has had its impact on capital asset prices (usually property) when banks collectively shift their behaviour, often in response to a new international opening, or deregulation of a market. After the launch of the euro, the creation of excessive cross-border credit by banks, taking advantage of low interest rates, pushed up real estate prices and private debt in so-called peripheral euro-zone countries (in particular Greece, Ireland, Spain and Portugal), but came to a sudden stop when the 2008 global financial crisis caused the same banks to curb their lending, resulting in a debt overhang and a prolonged euro-zone recession.

It has been suggested in Chapter Six that, as well as stability of real economy prices, a public policy objective of stability of financial and asset prices is desirable. Translated into the European sphere, this could mean national central banks, operating in a decentralised way through the European System of Central Banks, monitoring and keeping in check local asset prices. Since property is usually the most troublesome capital asset, yardsticks of long-term commercial real estate yields, such as are being developed for commercial property as collateral against bank loans in the UK, could be useful when judging whether credit-fuelled prices are becoming unstable. If so, commercial bank networks could be required to switch credit creation away from existing capital assets like property towards other activities, including financing business investment in new capital assets.

Looking ahead: post-crash economics in Europe

Against this background, a long-term European capital market, as outlined in this chapter, should improve European growth prospects by allowing a higher proportion of savings to move into investment in new capital assets. It should, in addition, help capital asset price stability by dampening speculation in short-term stock markets and trading platforms. Finally, a more sophisticated European macroeconomic policy could integrate a private investment initiative like this with other Europe-led investment expectations (like the Juncker Plan), and also the varied national Member State plans for public investment expenditure, including at local and regional level, which fall outside the central EU budget but constitute the bulk of public expenditure. This would mean that investment expectations would be better coordinated, and take account of one another.

One of the criticisms of traditional "Keynesian" stimulus plans is that, after a crisis, it is not easy to identify and start up completely new public sector investment projects, like infrastructure, to compensate for a sudden private sector downturn. A better method (and closer to Keynes' own thinking) would be to monitor both private and public investment expectations regularly, so that an aggregate picture of streams and flows of resources can be established. Public plans (which are invariably long-term and multi-annual) can then be accelerated or decelerated in light of expected private sector activity, to aim to ensure a consistent level of investment as a component of effective demand in Europe, and a sustainable level of growth.

If it is objected that this amounts to an unnecessary exercise in planning at a European level, it could be pointed out that the original Monnet Plan in France was also an investment plan (for the post-war economic modernisation of France); that it worked; and that there is no evidence whatsoever that such a coordination of expectations will organise itself. Unlike the price mechanism which operates in real economy markets for goods and services (or current output from existing capital assets), there exists no Hayekian coordination mechanism or telecommunications system that automatically brings dispersed knowledge of this nature together.

Rather than view the issue from an existing institutional or legal perspective, it might be better to work backwards from the problem which is to be solved, and think creatively about the means of doing so. The objective would be to have a higher proportion of European savings being used for private investment, through the medium of a long-term capital market; and also for public (or quasi-public) investment to have regard to expected levels of private investment. In fact, these two aspects are complementary: private companies generally find it easier to make long-term investment plans when they know what public intentions are; public authorities need to know there will be sufficient private investment coming on stream to maintain effective demand and growth.

An innovative pan-European approach might, then, involve a small institution (perhaps along the lines of the tiny body which serviced the original Monnet Plan, working *within* established governmental structures) whose task is to study and bring together existing plans for investment on a European scale. Some would be at EU level itself, such as from the European Investment Bank and EU budget expenditure programmes; much would be at EU Member State level, financed either through central government or through local and regional programmes;

some would be through other quasi-public or semi-private bodies like the national development banks (KfW), etc; and some – an increasing proportion over time – would be through the medium of a long-term capital market.

Having built up the best picture of investment plans over the next five or ten years, the way would then be open for those responsible for taking decisions to modulate, bring forward, or put back, multi-annual investment plans in line with the overall aggregate position. If private levels of investment are satisfactory, and asset prices are not appreciating, public schemes can be left to run on schedule. If private levels are insufficient (or are likely to be) public plans can be brought forward by a year or two, on an aggregate or else on a more targeted basis.

No element of compulsion, or additional public expenditure, should be necessary. The position would become one where long-term plans and expectations would have regard to other long-term plans, and how they fit into one another. The problem of dispersed knowledge – Hayek's problem – which resolves itself via the price mechanism for goods and services in the European single market, would in this way be addressed upstream for investment, or the creation of new capital assets, where the price mechanism is ineffective. Dispersed knowledge would be brought together, but in a different way, leaving those taking decisions subject to long-term expectation in a better position to do so; driven less by the "mass psychology of a large number of ignorant individuals" and more by knowledge of the overall needs of the European economy.

Notes

1. Kay J, *Other People's Money*, 2015, London, Profile Books, page 209.
2. "Report to the Annual General Meeting of the National Mutual", 1938, *Keynes Collected Writings*, Cambridge, Cambridge University Press, Vol XII, page 238.
3. Smithers A, *The Road to Recovery*, 2013, Chichester, John Wiley and Sons, page 95.
4. Shiller R, *Investor Behavior in the October 1987 Stock Market Crash: Survey Evidence*, 1987, NBER Working Paper No. 2446.
5. "Investing for Prosperity: Skills, Infrastructure and Innovation", *Report of the London School of Economics Growth Commission*, 2013 (www.lse.ac.uk).
6. Bogle J, "America's Financial System – Powerful but Flawed", 2010, lecture at Temple University, Philadelphia, Pennsylvania.
7. Haldane A, "The Age of Asset Management?", speech 2014, Bank of England.
8. Bogle J, *The Clash of the Cultures*, 2012, Hoboken, New Jersey, John Wiley and Sons, page 44.
9. *The Road to Recovery*, page 3.
10. de Larosière J, *Thoughts on Monetary Policy: A European Perspective*, 2016, Washington, Group of Thirty, Consultative Group on International Economic and Monetary Affairs.
11. Figures from Shin H, "How Much Should We Read into Shifts in Long-Dated Yields?", speech 2017, Bank for International Settlements; *Asset Management Market Study – Interim Report*, 2016, Financial Conduct Authority, London.
12. "How Much Should We Read into Shifts in Long-Dated Yields?".
13. Euro 2030, "Towards a true European Investment Fund", 2014 (http://en.euro2030.eu).
14. *Thoughts on Monetary Policy: A European Perspective*.
15. "Investing for Prosperity: Skills, Infrastructure and Innovation".

A new European capital market 99

16 Monnet J, *Memoirs*, 1978, New York, Doubleday, page 292.
17 *Comité Intergouvernemental Créé par la Conférence de Messine, Rapport des Chefs de Délégation aux Ministres des Affaires Etrangères*, Bruxelles, 21 April 1956, Archives nationales, Paris, Brochures doc Mae 120 (*Spaak Report*, translation by the author).
18 *Towards a Single Market in Financial Services*, 1992, European Commission Document 3/1992 in the European File Series.

9 Geopolitics

We saw in Chapter One how many different political developments around the world in the decades since the end of the Bretton Woods system in the 1970s can be interpreted in the light of successive waves of financial and economic crises. Political systems everywhere, of whatever type, have been tested and stressed by what appear, at the time, to be incomprehensible reversals of fortune. In some cases, societies cope stoically with a crisis; in other cases regimes change, and societies fracture. The inability of governments – whether elected or not – to provide assurance that they are in control of events, or can stop another crisis, has sapped confidence in politics.

In *World Order* (2014), Henry Kissinger suggests the political and the economic organisations of the world are at variance with each other. While political systems remain, mostly, national, economic organisation ignores national frontiers, and there is a global economic impetus to remove obstacles to the flow of goods and capital:

> This dynamic has produced decades of sustained economic growth punctuated by periodic financial crises of seemingly escalating intensity: in Latin America in the 1980s; in Asia in 1997; in Russia in 1998; in the United States in 2001 and then again starting in 2007; in Europe after 2010. [...] While each of those crises has had a different cause, their common feature has been profligate speculation and systemic underappreciation of risk. Financial instruments have been invented that obscure the nature of the relevant transactions. Lenders have found it difficult to estimate the extent of their commitments and borrowers, including major nations, to understand the implications of their indebtedness.[1]

As Kissinger describes it, the economic managers of globalisation have few occasions to engage with its political processes; and the managers of the political processes have few incentives to risk their domestic support on anticipating economic or financial problems the complexity of which eludes the understanding of all but experts.

This disjunction is dangerous. The experts continue to suggest things are not going well. Since the 2008 global financial crisis, economists at the IMF in 2017 have reported a sharp downturn in productivity growth across advanced, emerging and low-income countries around the world; and that decline, added to weak investment in advanced economies, has been the main contributor to output losses.[2] And at the Bank for International Settlements, the head of the Monetary and Economic Department has put forward the thesis that "financial cycle drag" helps explain the poor state of the global economy, with a sequence of large financial booms and busts over several decades causing huge and long-lasting economic damage.[3] As well as lost output following a crisis – bad though that is – there is a misallocation of resources in the boom preceding it, in particular towards lower-productivity growth sectors, like construction.

Meanwhile, the managers of political processes risk eviction, if they have the bad luck to be in office when a financial crisis hits. In their paper "Going to Extremes: Politics after Financial Crises, 1870–2014", Funke, Schularick and Trebesch have studied the political fall-out from financial crises in 20 developed countries over the past 140 years, and find that policy uncertainty rises strongly after financial crises as government majorities shrink and polarisation rises.[4] After a crisis, voters seem to be particularly attracted to the political rhetoric of the extreme right, often attributing blame to minorities or foreigners. On average, extreme right-wing parties increase their vote share by 30% after a financial crisis. The electoral gains of far-right parties have been particularly pronounced after the global economic crises of the 1920s/1930s, and again after 2008.

The dynamic is not difficult to understand. Competent government becomes extremely hard after a financial crisis; scapegoats are sought; establishments are rejected. But it is not as if far-right or extremist parties have the answers: financial crises repeat themselves unless action is taken at the root, which affects everyone. Far-right parties offer angry rhetoric, but no practical solutions.

After the global economic crisis of the 1920s and 1930s, and the Second World War, action at the root was taken and significant elements of post-war construction were put in place, in an effort to build a better global order. Prominent among those was the Bretton Woods monetary system, which, by and large, provided a stable framework for the expanding post-war world economy. One might see the irony in the fact that it was Nixon, Kissinger's own President, who triggered the demise of Bretton Woods by suspending the gold convertibility of the dollar in 1971. The world (including the US) has been paying the price ever since. (And, to be fair to Kissinger, it should be said he has on several occasions called for a return to a global regulatory system, or a new kind of Bretton Woods agreement.)[5]

How might we consider establishing a more stable geopolitical system, which does not spontaneously generate ever more intense financial crises, politically destructive and economically ruinous?

The two faces of globalisation

The argument of this book, derived from a Keynes/Minsky synthesis, can be summarised as follows. The future is always and necessarily open, and therefore uncertain, and economic processes involving capital investment and production take up time, which mean they too are subject to uncertainty. In the face of uncertainty, expectations exist, and these expectations are translated into prices in the market economy, but in two different ways.

In the first instance, when producers put items on the market for sale, in the shape of normal goods and services, their short-term expectations of what price they will achieve in relation to the costs they have incurred are confirmed (or not) when a sale takes place, and a purchaser agrees to buy the items at a given price. This price signalling process permeates throughout the whole economy, if it is competitive, and provides the basis of the division of labour, within a national economy and also internationally. Globalisation here increases the division of labour, leads to the creation of new goods and services and, generally, adds to the wealth of nations. It is a relatively stable system.

However, a second price system prevails in financial markets, which value the income flows from already existing financial and capital assets (including the assets used by producers to produce goods and services). Expectations of the income (yield) from the use of capital assets are much more long-term in nature than expectations of product prices, and there is no simple way of testing them through a direct price mechanism. They are inherently more volatile and unsteady. Instead, liquid investment markets provide prices, through the process of buying and selling securities giving rights to income flows. However, in the face of an uncertain future, these prices are often determined in practice less by attempting to make reasonable estimates of yields and more by attempting to establish the immediate view of other market participants. (This is the "speculation" Kissinger alludes to.)

The prices which result from the shifting of resources in liquid investment markets are volatile, and given to self-reinforcing booms and busts. They then feed back into the real economy by providing misleading signals for real capital investment (that is, the creation of new capital assets), over the long term eroding productivity and growth. The extension of credit is a variation on this theme: where existing capital assets (usually property) are used as collateral for credit, shifts in the collective expectations of inter-connected banks can cause excessive inflows of credit to push up the price of property, sudden stops in credit (revisions of opinion) and debt overhangs when prices drop.

Globalisation here therefore amounts to internationalising an inherently unstable system, to the point where it has now become a global (and therefore closed) system, misallocating resources in booms and busts, impeding the creation of new capital assets and, ultimately, eroding living standards.

Ominously, at some stage in recent decades, and certainly by the turn of the century, the volume of global transactions under the second, unstable, system overtook the volume under the first, stable, system.[6]

In both types of price system expectations precede prices. Where do expectations come from? As the philosopher of science Karl Popper has explained, all living creatures have expectations of the world in which they live, most of which are inborn and pre-conscious. It is the testing of expectations against reality which creates the growth of knowledge. It is only one small step from the amoeba to

Einstein. In human society, including the world of economics, expectations are usually based on previously observed regularities. The important question is not so much where expectations come from, but whether they can be tested, through a trial and error process. If so, knowledge is increased, and if (like Einstein, and unlike the amoeba) that knowledge can be transmitted to others, for example in the form of scientific theories, the total stock of human knowledge can increase.

In the first price system, the testing of expectations takes place through the trial and error process of the price mechanism. When producers put items on the market for sale, they may well have expectations, based on experience, of what price they will achieve, but they cannot know for sure until a purchaser agrees to pay a price. It may seem a bit of an exaggeration to say that the prices that emerge from this trial and error process constitute a form of knowledge: but that is exactly what Hayek suggested in 1945.[7] It may be only practical, not scientific or theoretical, knowledge, but it is useful knowledge all the same.

In the second price system, expectations are insufficiently tested through a trial and error process. They are reinforced, or shift, in the light of the collective opinion (Keynes called it a "*conventional basis of valuation*") in liquid markets where the dominant strategy is for everyone to try to anticipate what everyone else expects. This then creates a disconnect from the real world. Untested and shifting expectations remain stuck in a kind of pre-scientific or pseudo-scientific limbo, populated by the shades of half-formed narratives, factoids, myths and legends (for example, "countries don't go bankrupt"; "information technology changes everything"; "property prices never fall"). There is no increase in the stock of knowledge, in Hayek's sense. Instead, since communications are now instantaneous, and the system has become global, expectations form and shift like a radioactive cloud of unknowing, hovering in correlated ignorance over a world of uncertainty.

Reinforcing global stability

From the perspective of this two-price system, the elements of a more stable geopolitical order for globalisation might, however, be discerned. There is, first, little obviously wrong and requiring a radical overhaul with the first price system, involving real goods and services put on the market by producers for sale to purchasers. Competition policies can always be improved, to deal with new forms of concentration of producer power, the effects of global markets, and the impact of state-run or state-subsidised companies; but there is no need to impede the flow of goods and return to the disasters of protectionism of the pre-war decades, or to the command and control economies of the Soviet system.

It is the second price system where the difficulties lie. In an ideal world, there might be a proper formal "new Bretton Woods", which would learn from, and correct, the mistakes which led the first Bretton Woods system to fall apart. But even without that, action can still be taken (see the Technical Annex: "Do we really need a new Bretton Woods?"). The main point to appreciate is that this price system is inherently unstable, and there is no reason to expect it to correct itself. Although international currencies are part of the problem, the instability goes wider, and exists within economies as well as between them. On the other hand, the instability does not arise from malign intent, or the irredeemable wickedness of bankers. It arises, essentially, from an erroneous extension of transactions appropriate to the real economy to the financial system, which is valuing something completely different. Trading relations in the real economy do not correspond at all to what "traders" do in finance.

Since the second price system is unstable, the focus should be on making it more stable, using whatever public policy tools are available. In an open and uncertain world, public authorities have no more idea than anyone else what the future holds. It is precisely because of this that they need to maintain a balance, so that those in speculative financial markets who are (sometimes with vast resources) pushing a price in one direction do not overwhelm with momentum effects those who would push it in the opposite direction. Any departure from balance – which is price instability – can become dangerous, sooner or later. The action to be taken is therefore not to command or control the financial system, but to stop collective expectations from getting out of hand, before they can crystallise into prices having damaging effects in real economy markets. Such an approach would reinforce the many private sector initiatives around the world to curb short-termism and mis-pricing in finance, some mentioned in this book.

Since expectations of this nature tend to be based on previously observed regularities, a straightforward public policy of promoting financial and asset price stability, across the board and across the globe, would provide clarity, and anchor those expectations. This would include, for central banks, building on the mandate they already hold to maintain price stability in real economy markets (by targeting consumer price inflation) and extending it to the promotion of stable financial and capital asset prices. It would include, for financial regulators, building on the mandate they hold to maintain financial system stability (under the guidance of the post-crisis international Financial Stability Board), and including in that the instability of financial prices which undermine financial system stability. And it would include, for competition authorities, building on the mandate they already hold to keep real economy markets competitive (which is also conducive to price stability), and extending it to any anti-competitive behaviour in the second price system which undermines the public policy of price stability.

These institutions already exist around the world, and have many international networks of co-operation between them. What is required is that the stability of financial and asset prices should be recognised as a global public good, to which they should henceforth have regard.

Details will vary from market to market, including how to define price instability in relation to the underlying long-term yield of the asset in question, and how best to take action to achieve stability. Price stability would not mean a price freeze, or a price control: as in the real economy, aggregate stability would be the general objective, enabling individual price signals to become more meaningful (rather than, as too often at present, correlating with one another globally). If this appears an intolerable intrusion into the freedom of finance, it could be pointed out that the aim is to dampen down speculation, not to stop the creation of new capital assets, and that this speculation nearly always involves securities representing titles to already existing capital assets. By definition, it adds nothing to the stock of capital, or global growth.

Price stability as a global public good should also become easier to achieve if a unified co-operative approach is taken by public authorities. Since the second price system has become global, a global response is appropriate – and strengthens the hand of those applying it. Under the IMF Articles of Agreement, each IMF member is already committed to "seek to promote stability by fostering orderly underlying economic and financial conditions and a monetary system that does not tend to produce erratic disruptions".[8] Putting this commitment into practice becomes easier the more widely it is pursued.

What about global currencies, whose shifts are also driven by speculative markets? Stability here is certainly also desirable (and exchange stability remains to this day one of the purposes of the IMF).[9] While a purely dollar-based system, as under Bretton Woods, seems impossible to recreate today, there is good reason for co-operation between the major central banks by using intra-central bank money to create a more stable monetary order. That intra-central bank money could be based on gold, a basket of commodities or even the capital stock of the world. Relative currency stability would also help global trade, and if there are to be currency adjustments, reflecting changes in underlying economic reality, they should become much smoother, not sharply discontinuous.

Financial and asset price stability should have both economic and political benefits. In economic terms, price stability should, as in the real economy, mean a better allocation of resources, and less shifting of momentum flows of finance in and out of appreciating (and then depreciating) assets, frequently property-related. It should also encourage private sector real investment and productivity, the missing link in developed economies in recent decades, by allowing a smoother flow of savings seeking long-term steady returns into businesses seeking long-term investment capital. And, of course, price stability implies fewer disastrous financial crises, as the build-up of excessive financial and asset price appreciation would be curtailed.

In political terms, we have already seen that many political crises turn out to have an economic origin; and most economic crises have a financial origin. A more stable global financial system would therefore have geopolitical consequence: it would lead to less severe stress on existing social orders, and remove a potential source of conflict, and a potent source of extremism. More: a stable financial system could, as in the decades up to 1971, help put the world back on the trajectory of higher growth, in turn making it easier to address other urgent problems of world order – including writing down or rescheduling the overhang of debt built up since the disciplines of Bretton Woods were removed.

The open society and its enemies

When Keynes gave the closing speech moving to accept the Final Act of the Bretton Woods conference during the Second World War in 1944, he said that, if the constructive work started there could continue, "*this nightmare, in which most of us here present have spent too much of our lives, will be over*".[10] It seems incredible that, once again, far-right and extremist parties could be on the rise again, in the wake of modern financial crises.

Popper wrote *The Open Society and Its Enemies* in exile as his war-work in New Zealand, also during the Second World War, deciding to write it the day he learned in 1938 that Nazi Germany had invaded his native Austria. Popper wrote nothing at all about the war, but instead contemplated the tensions over two thousand years earlier in ancient Greece, when another philosopher (Plato) tried to make sense of the breakdown of his world caused by the war between the Greek city states of Athens and Sparta. We today, after another global economic crisis, can look back on Popper looking back on Plato.

Popper disagreed with Plato's solution, which was to see the problem of government as the answer to the question: *Who should rule? Who ought to be given power in the state?* To these questions, Plato's answer was: *The wise shall lead and rule, and the ignorant shall follow.* As Popper later put it:

> Later theorists of government, even those who disagreed with Plato's answer, still accepted Plato's formulation of the question. They too asked, like Plato, 'Who should rule?' and they gave various answers, such as 'the people' or 'the nation' or 'the master race'; in the case of Marx and the Marxists [...] the answer was: 'Not the capitalists, but the manual workers, that is, the proletariat.'
>
> Many theorists of democracy have also accepted Plato's question as correctly formulated, and since their answer was 'the people should rule' they developed a theory of democracy which was a theory of the sovereignty of the people.[11]

Popper disagreed with all this, and thought a better theory of the government of a free society would not start from the question: *Who should rule?* but rather: *How can we design our political institutions so that unwise or bad rulers do not obtain too much power, and cannot do too much damage?* In other words, we should take into account that rulers are often unwise, or worse, and there is no fool-proof method of selecting wise or good rulers. Democracy is valuable not because it throws up better or wiser leaders, but because it offers the chance of replacing bad ones.

Closed societies revert to the tribalism of pre-democratic ancient Greece, to which Plato wanted to return, with magical and collectivist tendencies. In Popper's book, "the magical or tribal or collectivist society will also be called the closed society, and the society in which individuals are confronted with personal decisions, the open society".[12]

Popper thought that when we say that our Western civilisation derives from the Greeks, this means that the Greeks started a revolution which is probably still in its infancy – the transition from the closed to the open society. But strains on society, arising from any number of factors, can always cause a wish to go backwards, back to the apparent security of the closed society, and back to the tribe.

This, then, is the explanation for the rise of the far-right, extremist (or tribal) parties after severe financial crises. Because the strains are global in nature, the wish is to retreat backward into a pre-global era, of tribal, closed collectives. It also explains the renewed emphasis on national "sovereignty" after a crisis, which is also a kind of magical thinking. As Popper put it:

> the idea of nationalism is a philosophical idea. It sprang from the theory of sovereignty – the theory that power in the state must be undivided – and from the idea of a superhuman ruler who rules by the grace of God. Rousseau's replacement of the king by the people only inverted the view: he made of the people a nation – a superhuman nation by the grace of God. Thus the theory of political nationalism originates in a philosophical inversion of the theory of absolute monarchy.[13]

The difficulty with seeking to regain "sovereignty" is that it is a mystical concept, reverting to the closed, magical, tribal, society. This may be comforting in the face of global crises and disorder, but it has nothing useful to contribute to solving global economic and financial problems. Superhuman rulers, or nations, will not make them disappear, as if by magic. Rather than relying on the archaic idea of national "sovereignty" the term "jurisdiction" would be better and more accurate for modern open societies, and reflects their law-abiding nature. A world of multiple jurisdictions can find lasting practical solutions to common problems: a world of multiple absolute sovereignties cannot.

And unless the problems are faced, and common solutions sought, Keynes' nightmare will not end.

A world of propensities

The fundamental difference between the Keynes/Minsky synthesis adopted in this book and much of mainstream financial economics in the post-war period is that the former accepts that the future is genuinely uncertain, and cannot be reduced to a simple probability analysis, or to a statistical calculation of risks. As a consequence, mathematical calculations and models which try to do so, whether relied on by investors, financial institutions, central banks or regulators, are likely to be dangerously simplistic and misleading.

In Popper's terms, an open society permits peaceful, non-violent change. Not only is the future course of human history not determined; but the subjects themselves of the natural and physical sciences are also open and indeterminate. The universe itself is open.

If we accept, with Popper, the unity of method between the social and natural sciences, we can also see that the Keynes/Minsky approach has the merit of putting economics on the same footing as other social and natural sciences, all of which face the same problem of creating testable or falsifiable theories which better explain a profoundly mysterious universe. Perhaps this is what Keynes had in mind when he said classical economic theory might work very well in a world in which economic goods are consumed within a short interval of being produced (in other words, the first price system, above), but that it needs considerable amendment the further the accumulation of wealth is postponed into an indefinite and uncertain future.

The existence of uncertainty does not mean that better theories cannot find better explanations and ways of predicting events, so that knowledge can grow, as in other social and natural sciences. But it means that this is not a simple statistical exercise, and that what works in short-term transactions involved in the production of goods (or wealth used) does not explain what happens when wealth is postponed. Keynes was worried about the "dark forces of time and ignorance" which envelop our future, and which threaten to overwhelm skilled investment. On the other hand, shedding light on darkness has been the goal and achievement of science since the Greek foundations of our Western science and civilisation over two thousand years ago.

In Popper's late writings there is a tantalising glimpse of a movement beyond classical probability theory to a theory of propensities – a world of propensities.[14] Propensities are weighted possibilities, affecting statistical probabilities, resulting from minute changes in the very properties of the physical situation where an event occurs. A slightly loaded or weighted die will have non-equal possibilities of landing on one of its six faces, with a propensity affecting the statistical results when it is rolled. In a scientific experiment, it is necessary to exclude interfering propensities, or disturbing extraneous influences such as changes of temperature or of the normal moisture of the air, if we want to create results that can be repeated at will. But that is very difficult to do, and hardly ever happens outside artificial laboratory conditions, or rare natural laboratories such as isolated planetary systems.

Popper came to think that propensities themselves are real, like attractive forces, pulling on possibilities, allowing them to realise themselves. In this way, new possibilities are created. The "possibility space" (the space of non-zero possibilities) is growing:

> And behind this growth there seems to be hidden something like a natural law that can be stated as follows: All non-zero possibilities, even those to which only a tiny non-zero propensity is attached, will realize themselves in time, provided they have time to do so: that is to say, provided the conditions repeat themselves sufficiently often or remain constant over a sufficiently long period of time.[15]

A world of propensities is therefore not deterministic or mechanistic at all. It is growing. The past is closed but the future is open. It is practically impossible to keep all the probabilistically relevant conditions constant – except perhaps in some laboratory experiments, or perhaps in outer space.

Two concluding remarks flow from this. The first is that, as Keynes said, the material of economics here on this earth cannot be constant and homogenous. It has to do with *"motives, expectations, psychological uncertainties"*. In the *General Theory*, the title of Book III is "The *Propensity* to Consume". The title of Book IV is "The *Inducement* to Invest". To speak in propensities is to speak in a richer language than probabilities. Keynes accused orthodox economic theory, resting upon the wrong hypothesis of a calculable future, of being "one equation short of what is required to give a solution". The solutions found in the laboratory experiments of economic models running in a perpetual present will always be one dimension short of reality.

The second remark is that, with the addition of the dimension of time, even faint possibilities will realise themselves. If the world can be kept open, and stable, more possibilities will appear. From the tiny city states of Greece to today's gigantic global economy, the choice is always whether the right standards, rules and institutions can be found to solve the problems of the present, and let the possibilities of the future have time and scope to emerge.

Notes

1. Kissinger H, *World Order*, 2014, 2015, London, Penguin Random House, page 368.
2. Adler G, Duval R, Furceri D, Çelik S, Koloskovaka K and Poplawski-Ribeiro M, "Gone with the Headwinds: Global Productivity", 2017, IMF Staff Discussion Note.
3. Borio C, "Secular Stagnation or Financial Cycle Drag?", 2017, Keynote Speech at the US National Association for Business Economics Conference (www.bis.org).
4. Funke, M, Schularick M and Trebesch C, "Going to Extremes: Politics after Financial Crises, 1870–2014", *European Economic Review*, 2016, 88, C: pages 227–260.
5. In, for example, "The Chance for a New World Order", Henry Kissinger article, *International Herald Tribune*, 12 January 2009.
6. *US Treasury Report to Congress on International Economic and Exchange Rate Policies*, 2007, Appendix 1: Cross Border Capital Flows and Foreign Exchange Market Activities.
7. Hayek F, "The Use of Knowledge in Society", 1945, *American Economic Review.*
8. Article IV, Section 1 (ii), Articles of Agreement of the International Monetary Fund, last amended 2010 (www.imf.org).
9. Article I (iii), IMF Articles of Agreement.
10. Conway E, *The Summit*, 2014, London, Little Brown, page 280.
11. Shearmur J and Turner P (Eds.), *After The Open Society*, 2008, 2012, Abingdon, Routledge, page 242.
12. Popper K, *The Open Society and Its Enemies*, 1971, Princeton, New Jersey, Princeton University Press, page 173.
13. Popper K, *The Myth of the Framework*, 1994, 1996, London, Routledge, page 186.
14. Popper K, *A World of Propensities*, 1990, 1995, Bristol, Thoemmes Press.
15. *A World of Propensities*, page 19.

Technical annex
Do we really need a new Bretton Woods?

This technical annex attempts a preliminary answer to a question often raised, which is whether a new Bretton Woods is necessary or desirable.

The ending of the post-war Bretton Woods system is usually taken to mean the suspension of the gold convertibility of the US dollar in 1971. Since then, the dollar has no longer been tied to gold, and other currencies have floated independently, with fluctuating values set in international foreign exchange markets.

It has been suggested in this book that there are general benefits in relatively stable financial and asset prices, and that this objective could be pursued as a global public good, by a number of different methods.

To what extent would this require a new Bretton Woods? Or can the existing Bretton Woods system be used instead?

Currency stability

Despite the suspension of the dollar/gold link, currency stability remains a formal objective of the Bretton Woods system. One of the purposes of the International Monetary Fund, as set out in its Articles of Agreement, is to "promote exchange stability, to maintain orderly exchange arrangements among members, and to avoid competitive exchange depreciation" (Article I (iii)).

Each member of the IMF also remains formally subject to the Article IV Obligations Regarding Exchange Arrangements. The general obligations, set out in Section 1, are as follows:

> Recognizing that the essential purpose of the international monetary system is to provide a framework that facilitates the exchange of goods, services and capital among countries, and that sustains sound economic growth, and that a principal objective is the continuing development of the orderly underlying conditions that are necessary for financial and economic stability, each member undertakes to collaborate with the Fund and other members to assure orderly exchange arrangements and to promote a stable system of exchange rates. In particular, each member shall:
>
> (i) endeavor to direct its economic and financial policies toward the objective of fostering orderly economic growth with reasonable price stability, with due regard to its circumstances;

(ii) seek to promote stability by fostering orderly underlying economic and financial conditions and a monetary system that does not tend to produce erratic disruptions;
(iii) avoid manipulating exchange rates or the international monetary system in order to prevent effective balance of payments adjustment or to gain an unfair competitive advantage over other members; and
(iv) follow exchange policies compatible with the undertakings under this Section.

In other words, the global legal framework, as set out in the Articles of Agreement of the IMF, last amended in 2010 but first adopted in 1944, and then ratified by the governments of countries around the world, is one where the principle of collaboration to promote a stable system of exchange rates still exists.

For there to be a worldwide system, a high majority is required. According to Article IV Section 2 (c), to have "general exchange agreements" between IMF members there needs to be an 85% majority of the total voting power of the IMF. And according to Article IV Section 4, the IMF "may determine, by an eighty-five per cent majority of the total voting power, that international economic conditions permit the introduction of a widespread system of exchange arrangements based on stable but adjustable par values."

However, other more limited arrangements are possible. Under Article IV Section 2 (b),

> exchange arrangements may include (i) the maintenance by a member of a value for its currency in terms of the special drawing right or another denominator, other than gold, selected by the member, or (ii) cooperative arrangements by which members maintain the value of their currencies in relation to the value of the currency or currencies of other members, or (iii) other exchange arrangements of a member's choice.

The last option explains why today's "non-system" can exist. But regional currency arrangements – such as the euro – are also consistent with IMF rules. So would be arrangements for greater currency stability between a core of two or three global currencies (as suggested by Robert Mundell for the US dollar, the euro and the Chinese yuan).

At first sight, the prohibition on maintaining a currency value based on gold seems a stumbling block. But this could be circumvented by using a denominator that includes gold (such as a basket of commodities), or a completely different denominator (such as Pringle's real assets). Keynes' "bancor" (central bank gold) might also fall outside the prohibition.

Greater currency stability does not therefore appear to require a new Bretton Woods: only that the spirit and the rules of the existing Bretton Woods system are applied more widely.

Asset price stability

The Articles of Agreement of the IMF do not distinguish between real economy prices and asset prices. But Article IV, as noted above, commits each member to the objective of fostering orderly economic growth "with reasonable price stability". It also commits each member to seek to promote stability "by fostering orderly underlying economic and financial conditions and a monetary system that does not tend to produce erratic disruptions".

Greater co-operation to foster orderly underlying financial conditions, and to reverse the tendency of today's monetary system to produce very great "erratic disruptions" in the shape of financial crises, is therefore squarely within the Article IV objective.

The solution suggested in this book – action by authorities like central banks, financial regulators and competition authorities around the world to ensure asset prices are more stable, because based on underlying yields – appears in the spirit of Article IV. Moreover, under Article IV Section 3 (a) the IMF has the duty of overseeing the international monetary system in order to ensure its effective operation, and the compliance of each member with its obligations. The IMF is also supposed to promote international monetary co-operation through a permanent institution "which provides the machinery for consultation and collaboration on international monetary problems". The IMF could, therefore, oversee decentralised action by public authorities intended to promote stability.

So seeking asset price stability is not an explicit Bretton Woods objective. But reasonable stability does appear compatible with the objectives of fostering orderly financial conditions and a non-erratic monetary system. Again, a new Bretton Woods may not be necessary: merely enforcing existing agreements.

Global investment and productivity

Also within the Bretton Woods system is the World Bank. It is worth noting that according to the Articles of Agreement of the World Bank (also adopted in 1944 and most recently amended in 2012), the purposes of the Bank include Article I (iii):

> To promote the long-range balanced growth of international trade and the maintenance of equilibrium in balances of payments by encouraging international investment for the development of the productive resources of members, thereby assisting in raising productivity, the standard of living and conditions of labor in their territories.

A global financial system less devoted to speculation and more devoted to investment for the development of productive resources and raising productivity and the standard of living would, once more, be compatible with the existing Bretton Woods agreements.

Effective demand

Connected to the Bretton Woods system was the idea of increasing international trade in the post-war period. The preamble to the World Trade Organization Agreement of 1994, largely based on the post-war General Agreement on Tariffs and Trade of 1947, begins with wording as follows:

The Parties to this Agreement

> Recognizing that their relations in the field of trade and economic endeavour should be conducted with a view to raising standards of living, ensuring full employment and a large and steadily growing volume of real income and effective demand, and expanding the production of and trade in goods and services…

"Effective demand", as mentioned here in relation to world trade, consists of two components: consumption expenditure and investment expenditure. Of these, it is investment which is the most prone to sudden and wide fluctuations, and which, therefore, is the key variable. An insufficient, or erratic, flow of savings into investment will cause the economy to underperform (or have what Keynes once called "magneto trouble"), depressing growth and employment. Again, the original objectives of increasing international trade appear to have been lost sight of.

A preliminary answer to the eternal question

Much might yet be done within the existing Bretton Woods system, which, on paper at least, aims at international currency stability; orderly financial conditions; a monetary system not subject to erratic disruptions; reasonable price stability; international investment for the development of productive resources and raising productivity; and steadily growing income and effective demand.

That none of these things now exist, and that, on the contrary, the world has experienced successive waves of financial and economic crises (*Cinquante Ans de Crises Financières*, as the laconic title of Jacques de Larosière's 2016 book has it), does not mean the objectives are wrong. It merely means the world has wandered far off the path of wisdom. But there seems no need to begin the search for wisdom all over again. It can be found already, at least on paper. For it to be put back to work may appear a huge task. Fifty years of crisis will not be reversed overnight. Nonetheless, a revived or modernised Bretton Woods could be an effective global response to the defects of today's globalisation.

Index

Alchemy of Finance, The (book) 34
All Life is Problem Solving (book) 12
American Recovery and Reinvestment Act (2009) 69
anti-competitive behaviour 16, 17, 73–74, 76
antitrust policy 16, 73
Articles of Agreement of the IMF 67, 70–71, 105, 110–111
asset management and price stability 78–80
asset price instability 60–62, 68, 112
Austrian banking cartel 73–74, 76
Authers, John 81

"bancor" 66, 111
Bank for International Settlements, the 22, 101
banking deregulation 4
banking in the European Single market 96
banking regulation and credit 34–35, 63–64
bank lending 88–89; and competition law 77, 96
bases of currency value 111
behaviour of institutional investors and rationality 50
Big Bang in the UK stock exchange, the 86–87
Bogle, John 31–32, 40, 58, 79, 89, 90
Bretton Woods monetary and financial system, the 2, 4, 57, 65, 95, 105–106, 112–113; as a stable framework 7, 56, 60, 101
British Business Bank, the 70
business ownership and management 84–85, 86

Caisse des Depots 70
Canada Pension Plan Investment Board, the 58

Capital in the Twenty-First Century (book) 24, 56, 61
capital investment: and future expected yield 20–21, 23–24, 27–29, 37–38; and uncertainty 20–22, 88
capital markets for long-term European investment requirements 89, 90–94, 96–97
capital raising and share valuations 85, 89
cartels and anti-competitive behaviour 16, 73–74, 76
Cassa Depositi e Prestiti 70
central banks 62–63, 64, 67, 104, 105
Cinquante Ans de Crises Financières (book) 113
closed banking systems 82
commercial real estate yields and financial stability 96
common European market, the 94–97
competition in the banking sector 74–77
competition law and policy 19, 73–74, 77–78, 80, 82–83, 95; and globalisation 80–81, 103
"conventional basis of valuation," phenomenon 59–60
corrective shifts in finance markets 57
correlations in global asset prices 81–82
credit and banking regulation 34–35, 63–64
credit bubbles 3, 4, 5–6, 26, 77, 96; in the property sector 56, 63, 64, 74
credit extensions 26, 102
currency fluctuation 4, 26, 55, 64–65, 81
currency stability 65, 67, 95, 105, 110–111, 113
currency trading 26–27

databases of previous long-term yields 91, 92
deregulation of financial markets 4, 77, 96

dispersed ownership of stock, the 85
division of labour, the 24, 29, 73, 82, 94, 102; and the price mechanism in the market economy 1, 13, 15–16
DSGE ("dynamic stochastic general equilibrium") model of economic forecasting 44

East India Company, the 84
ECB (European Central Bank), the 69
economic growth since the abandonment of a global monetary standard 6, 55
economic theories 7–8
effective demand and world trade 113
"Efficient Capital Markets: A Review of Theory and Empirical Work" (paper) 24–25
efficient market hypothesis and stock prices, the 24–25
Einstein, Albert 12, 103
Ellis, Charles 79
End of Alchemy, The (book) 11
entrepreneurs and uncertainty 13–14
ETFs (exchange traded funds) 40
EU, the 16
European Coal and Steel Community, the 73, 94
European households and equity investments 92–93
European Investment Bank, the 70, 88, 89, 95
European Monetary System, the 4, 5, 95
European Savings Account, proposal for a 93
European single market, the 5
Eurozone debt crisis, the 74–75
"evolutionary theory of knowledge," development of an 11–12
expectations 44, 56, 60, 62–63, 82, 87, 101–102; and knowledge and reality 12, 15, 21, 22–23, 48, 102–103; and "rational expectations" theory 46–49, 50; stabilisation of 42, 49; *see also* long-term expectation and investment decisions; scientific theory and expectation; uncertainty
expectations and the price mechanism 13–16, 17–19, 27, 33–34, 102–103; in financial markets 33–34, 102, 104; and prospective yield 28, 29, 102
Exxon Mobil 39

Fama, Eugene 24, 29
Fearful Rise of Markets, The (book) 81

Federal Reserve, the 63
fiduciary duties 58, 68
financial crises 101, 106, 107, 113; *see also* global financial crisis of 2007–08, the
financial divergence from economic reality 2–3
financial innovation 4
financial instability 9, 60, 95
financial regulation 35, 49, 67–68, 92; in the UK 48, 68, 74
financial stability 96, 111–112; and yield forecasting 42–43, 62, 79, 90, 91
Financial Stability Board, the 68
fixed stock exchange commissions 86–87
"Flash Crash" of 2010, the 88
floating exchange rate mechanisms 26, 55, 95
foreign exchange markets 34
free movement of capital, the 82, 95; and the geopolitical dynamic towards 100–101, 105–107
future expected yield from capital investment 20–21, 23–24, 27–29, 37–38
future income flows and the price system 2

GATT (General Agreement on Tariffs and Trade), the 112
General Theory of Employment, Interest and Money, The (book) 20, 28, 35, 45, 64, 84–85, 109; on expectations in an uncertain future 14–15, 19–20, 78, 86; on the long-term yields of capital assets 21, 23, 28; on speculation 21, 31, 40, 41; on the trade cycle and market correction 57, 86; *see also* Keynes, John Maynard
geopolitical dynamic towards free movement of goods and capital 100–101, 105–107
global financial crisis of 2007–08, the 6, 57, 74, 81, 88, 96, 100–101
globalisation: of competition policy 80–81, 103; and instability 102, 103–104
global network of national competition authorities 16–17
"Going to Extremes: Politics after Financial Crises, 1870–2014" (paper) 101
gold as a global monetary standard 2, 3, 6, 65–66, 101, 110; uncertainty generated since its abandonment 8–9, 55, 100
Greenspan, Alan 22, 53, 63

Index

Harrod, Roy 52
Hayek, Friedrich 15–16, 42, 76, 86, 98
heavy industry and competition policy 73
Howe, Geoffrey 7

Iceland 6
IMF (International Monetary Fund), the 67, 70–71, 100–101, 105, 110–111, 112
inflation 1–2, 3
institutional savings and investment since the war 86–87
insurance in a European single market 95–96
inter-bank market, the 34
interest rates 4, 26, 62–63, 88–89
International Competition Network, the 17
international monetary currency system alternatives 65–67, 70–71
International Trade Organisation treaty, the 16
intra-central bank money and financial stability 105
intra-financial system assets and liabilities 76
investment and capital assets 28–29
investment in long-term capital markets 91–92
investment markets 25, 31, 34, 88
investment planning in the UK 69–70
investment shortfalls since the financial crisis 69, 93, 97–98
IS-LM ("investment, savings - liquidity, money") macroeconomic model of economic forecasting 44
Issing, Otmar 69

"Juncker Plan" for infrastructure, the 93, 97

Kay, John 28, 69, 84, 88
Kay Review of UK Equity Markets and Long-Term Decision Making 69
Keynes, John Maynard 26, 52, 65–66, 75–76, 82, 105–106; on future uncertainty 7–8, 9, 50, 53–54, 103, 108; on investment 24, 25, 37; on liquidity 35–36; on shifts in the prices of assets 22, 56, 69; on speculation 89, 90; on the state role in public investment 42, 69, 97; on the stock market 22, 29; *see also General Theory of Employment, Interest and Money, The* (book)
Keynesianism, meaning of 57–58
KfW bank 70, 89
King, Mervyn 11, 23, 44

Kissinger, Henry 100, 101
Knight, Frank 7, 9, 13–14, 29, 48
knowledge and expectations against reality 12, 15, 21, 22–23, 48, 102–103
knowledge of the value of companies 86, 89, 91, 98

Larosière, Jacques de 56, 92, 93, 113
Latin American debt crisis, the 74
League of Nations, the 16
Lehman Brothers 6
liquid investment markets 35, 49, 102
liquidity 35–36
Logic of Scientific Discovery, The (book) 23
London Stock Exchange, the 84, 87
Long-Term Capital Management 5
long-term expectation and investment decisions 19–24, 27, 29, 42, 48
long-term investment measures to avoid short-termism in finance 58–61

Man Who Knew, The (book) 63
Map and the Territory, The (book) 53
marginal efficiency of capital, the 60
market economy, the 7, 13–15, 16
market making 87
Marx, Karl 106
Minsky, Hyman 2, 8, 22; on financial instability 21, 42; and "Money Manager Capitalism" 31, 55, 61, 89
models as applications of theories 45, 46–48
"momentum" trading 9, 32, 56, 61
"money manager capitalism" 31, 55, 61, 89
Money Trap, The (book) 66
Monnet, Jean 94
Monti, Mario 73
Mundell, Robert 67, 111
Muth, John 46–47
mutual funds 31, 32, 40, 89

nationalism as a philosophical idea 107
natural and social sciences, the 44–45, 48, 49–50, 107
new Bretton Woods economic and monetary system 103–105, 110–113
Newton, Sir Isaac 51
Newtonian theory of gravity as a universal force of attraction 51–52
Nixon, Richard 2, 6, 101

oil prices since the 1970s 3, 95
open market economy and the open society, the 17–18

open societies and government 105–107, 109
Open Society and Its Enemies, The (book) 7, 106
output and employment fluctuations 69

passive investment 40–41
pension funds 37, 39, 79, 89
physical investment financing 28, 39
Piketty, Thomas 24; *see also Capital in the Twenty-First Century* (book)
Plato 106
political economy of the global financial order, the 1
political extremism and financial crises 101, 106, 107
pooled funds and savings 31, 36, 37, 39, 61, 89, 92
Popper, Karl 7, 8, 9, 33, 106–107; and the natural and social sciences 33, 44–47, 50, 54; on propensities as possibilities 51–52, 53, 108; and "rational expectations" theory 46–49, 50; and theory of knowledge and future expectation 11–13, 15, 18, 23, 34, 38–39, 102
Posner, Richard 74
post-war economic modernisation and planning 73, 94, 95, 97
Poverty of Historicism, The (book) 44
price fixing 73
price mechanism, the 1–2; in the market economy 13–15, 17–18, 49, 73, 94–95, 97
prices and income controls 4
price stability 62–64, 67–69, 70, 77–80, 82–83, 103–105
Pringle, Robert 66–67
propensities as possible outcomes 52, 53, 108–109
property and long-term valuations 23, 26, 64
property price bubbles 56, 63, 64, 74
psychology of the market, the 23, 25, 29, 58, 77, 85
public debt levels and Keynesian deficit solutions 70
public expenditure and shortfalls in private investment 69
public utilities and long-term valuations 23
Putin, Vladimir 5

"radical uncertainty" and economic theory 11
rational and irrational behaviour in economics and universal laws of attraction 50–54

rational expectations in an efficient market economy 8, 24, 49
"rational expectations" theory 46–49, 50
rationality and the social sciences 45–46
real economy prices and financial prices 29, 34, 111–112
real estate prices 5–6
reflexive processes and expectations 33
"reflexivity" theory and expectations 27, 31, 32–33, 44
remunerations and investment decisions 25–26, 56, 61
research and development levels since the financial crisis 93
resource allocation in the capital market 24–25, 82
Risk, Uncertainty and Profit (book) 13
risk and speculation 85
risk transfer and future returns 23, 64
Roosa, Robert 26, 56
Russian economy, the 5

savings and investment 28, 37–38, 39, 41, 92–93; institutional nature of in the post-war period 31, 32, 36
scientific and non-scientific demarcations 12–13
scientific theory and expectation 12–13, 18, 107–108; and trial and error methods and the testing of expectations 22, 36, 38–39, 42–43, 49, 73, 86; and the growth of knowledge 12, 13, 15–16, 34, 103
securities and the price mechanism 1
shareholding values and company performance 89–91
share revaluations and daily fluctuations 20, 85
Shiller, Robert 87
short-term stock market speculation 32, 36, 37, 40–41, 55–56
short-term time horizons 37–38
Single European Act (1987), the 95
Smith, Adam 13, 73, 94
Smithers, Andrew 25, 59, 60, 87
Soros, George 27, 31, 32–34, 44
Soviet economy, the 4, 7
Spaak Report, the 94, 95
speculation 25, 27, 68, 77, 85; Keynes on 21, 31, 40, 41, 89, 90; in the short-term 32, 36, 37, 40–41, 55–56
S & P Long-Term Value Creation Global Index 58
Stabilising an Unstable Economy (book) 21

Standard Oil 73
Standard & Poor 500 Index, the 40
state and the allocation of economic investment, the 41–42
stock market crash (1987), the 87
stock markets 84–85; and trading volumes 25, 31–32, 79, 86, 87–88
stock prices 24–25, 62, 69
sub-prime mortgage market, the 6

theories of government 106
theory of finance, a 36–39, 44
theory of relativity, the 51
trading volumes on the stock market 25, 79, 86, 87, 88
Treatise on Money, A (book) 66, 75–76
Treaty of Rome (1957), the 73, 94, 95
Turner review of the UK Financial Services Authority 48

UK competition policy 74
UK economy, the 4, 5
UK Financial Conduct Authority, the 79
uncertainty 101–102, 107, 108; and the price mechanism 13–14, 17, 29–30, 53, 102; since the abandonment of a fixed global monetary standard 8–9, 55, 100; in the world of finance 36–37, 42–43, 50, 56, 59–60, 82, 101; *see also* expectations

"unity of scientific method" across the sciences 33, 34, 35, 44, 49–50
US anti-trust policy 16, 73
US dollar and gold, the 6, 65, 101, 110; *see also* gold as a global monetary standard
US Dow Jones, the 88
US institutional savings 31, 39, 40, 86
US stock market crash (1987) 63

Vanguard 31, 40
Vision for Real Estate Finance in the UK, a (report) 64
volatility in international prices 3, 16
Volcker, Paul 56, 65

wage inequality 61
Wall Street crash, the 86, 87
Woolley, Paul 32, 37, 39, 56, 59, 79
World Bank, the 112
World Order (book) 100
World Trade Organization Agreement (1994), the 112–113

yield forecasting: and capital assets 20–21, 23–24, 27–29, 37–38; databases of previous long-term yields 91, 92; and expectations and the price mechanism 28, 29, 102; and financial stability 42–43, 62, 79, 90, 91